FRENCH
VOCABULARY

ENGLISH-FRENCH

The most useful words
To expand your lexicon and sharpen
your language skills

5000 words

French vocabulary for English speakers - 5000 words

By Andrey Taranov

T&P Books vocabularies are intended for helping you learn, memorize and review foreign words. The dictionary is divided into themes, covering all major spheres of everyday activities, business, science, culture, etc.

The process of learning words using T&P Books' theme-based dictionaries gives you the following advantages:

- Correctly grouped source information predetermines success at subsequent stages of word memorization
- Availability of words derived from the same root allowing memorization of word units (rather than separate words)
- Small units of words facilitate the process of establishing associative links needed for consolidation of vocabulary
- Level of language knowledge can be estimated by the number of learned words

T&P Books Publishing
www.tpbooks.com

ISBN: 978-1-78071-303-8

This book is also available in E-book formats.
Please visit www.tpbooks.com or the major online bookstores.

FRENCH VOCABULARY
for English speakers

T&P Books vocabularies are intended to help you learn, memorize, and review foreign words. The vocabulary contains over 5000 commonly used words arranged thematically.

- Vocabulary contains the most commonly used words
- Recommended as an addition to any language course
- Meets the needs of beginners and advanced learners of foreign languages
- Convenient for daily use, revision sessions, and self-testing activities
- Allows you to assess your vocabulary

Special features of the vocabulary

- Words are organized according to their meaning, not alphabetically
- Words are presented in three columns to facilitate the reviewing and self-testing processes
- Words in groups are divided into small blocks to facilitate the learning process
- The vocabulary offers a convenient and simple transcription of each foreign word

The vocabulary has 155 topics including:

Basic Concepts, Numbers, Colors, Months, Seasons, Units of Measurement, Clothing & Accessories, Food & Nutrition, Restaurant, Family Members, Relatives, Character, Feelings, Emotions, Diseases, City, Town, Sightseeing, Shopping, Money, House, Home, Office, Working in the Office, Import & Export, Marketing, Job Search, Sports, Education, Computer, Internet, Tools, Nature, Countries, Nationalities and more ...

T&P BOOKS' THEME-BASED DICTIONARIES

The Correct System for Memorizing Foreign Words

Acquiring vocabulary is one of the most important elements of learning a foreign language, because words allow us to express our thoughts, ask questions, and provide answers. An inadequate vocabulary can impede communication with a foreigner and make it difficult to understand a book or movie well.

The pace of activity in all spheres of modern life, including the learning of modern languages, has increased. Today, we need to memorize large amounts of information (grammar rules, foreign words, etc.) within a short period. However, this does not need to be difficult. All you need to do is to choose the right training materials, learn a few special techniques, and develop your individual training system.

Having a system is critical to the process of language learning. Many people fail to succeed in this regard; they cannot master a foreign language because they fail to follow a system comprised of selecting materials, organizing lessons, arranging new words to be learned, and so on. The lack of a system causes confusion and eventually, lowers self-confidence.

T&P Books' theme-based dictionaries can be included in the list of elements needed for creating an effective system for learning foreign words. These dictionaries were specially developed for learning purposes and are meant to help students effectively memorize words and expand their vocabulary.

Generally speaking, the process of learning words consists of three main elements:

- Reception (creation or acquisition) of a training material, such as a word list
- Work aimed at memorizing new words
- Work aimed at reviewing the learned words, such as self-testing

All three elements are equally important since they determine the quality of work and the final result. All three processes require certain skills and a well-thought-out approach.

New words are often encountered quite randomly when learning a foreign language and it may be difficult to include them all in a unified list. As a result, these words remain written on scraps of paper, in book margins, textbooks, and so on. In order to systematize such words, we have to create and continually update a "book of new words." A paper notebook, a netbook, or a tablet PC can be used for these purposes.

This "book of new words" will be your personal, unique list of words. However, it will only contain the words that you came across during the learning process. For example, you might have written down the words "Sunday," "Tuesday," and "Friday." However, there are additional words for days of the week, for example, "Saturday," that are missing, and your list of words would be incomplete. Using a theme dictionary, in addition to the "book of new words," is a reasonable solution to this problem.

The theme-based dictionary may serve as the basis for expanding your vocabulary.

It will be your big "book of new words" containing the most frequently used words of a foreign language already included. There are quite a few theme-based dictionaries available, and you should ensure that you make the right choice in order to get the maximum benefit from your purchase.

Therefore, we suggest using theme-based dictionaries from T&P Books Publishing as an aid to learning foreign words. Our books are specially developed for effective use in the sphere of vocabulary systematization, expansion and review.

Theme-based dictionaries are not a magical solution to learning new words. However, they can serve as your main database to aid foreign-language acquisition. Apart from theme dictionaries, you can have copybooks for writing down new words, flash cards, glossaries for various texts, as well as other resources; however, a good theme dictionary will always remain your primary collection of words.

T&P Books' theme-based dictionaries are specialty books that contain the most frequently used words in a language.

The main characteristic of such dictionaries is the division of words into themes. For example, the *City* theme contains the words "street," "crossroads," "square," "fountain," and so on. The *Talking* theme might contain words like "to talk," "to ask," "question," and "answer".

All the words in a theme are divided into smaller units, each comprising 3–5 words. Such an arrangement improves the perception of words and makes the learning process less tiresome. Each unit contains a selection of words with similar meanings or identical roots. This allows you to learn words in small groups and establish other associative links that have a positive effect on memorization.

The words on each page are placed in three columns: a word in your native language, its translation, and its transcription. Such positioning allows for the use of techniques for effective memorization. After closing the translation column, you can flip through and review foreign words, and vice versa. "This is an easy and convenient method of review – one that we recommend you do often."

Our theme-based dictionaries contain transcriptions for all the foreign words. Unfortunately, none of the existing transcriptions are able to convey the exact nuances of foreign pronunciation. That is why we recommend using the transcriptions only as a supplementary learning aid. Correct pronunciation can only be acquired with the help of sound. Therefore our collection includes audio theme-based dictionaries.

The process of learning words using T&P Books' theme-based dictionaries gives you the following advantages:

- You have correctly grouped source information, which predetermines your success at subsequent stages of word memorization

- Availability of words derived from the same root (lazy, lazily, lazybones), allowing you to memorize word units instead of separate words

- Small units of words facilitate the process of establishing associative links needed for consolidation of vocabulary

- You can estimate the number of learned words and hence your level of language knowledge

- The dictionary allows for the creation of an effective and high-quality revision process

- You can revise certain themes several times, modifying the revision methods and techniques

- Audio versions of the dictionaries help you to work out the pronunciation of words and develop your skills of auditory word perception

The T&P Books' theme-based dictionaries are offered in several variants differing in the number of words: 1.500, 3.000, 5.000, 7.000, and 9.000 words. There are also dictionaries containing 15,000 words for some language combinations. Your choice of dictionary will depend on your knowledge level and goals.

We sincerely believe that our dictionaries will become your trusty assistant in learning foreign languages and will allow you to easily acquire the necessary vocabulary.

TABLE OF CONTENTS

PRONUNCIATION GUIDE

Letter	French example	T&P phonetic alphabet	English example

Vowels

Letter	French example	T&P phonetic alphabet	English example
A a	cravate	[a]	shorter than in ask
E e	mer	[ɛ]	man, bad
I i [1]	hier	[j]	yes, New York
I i [2]	musique	[i]	shorter than in feet
O o	porte	[o], [ɔ]	drop, baught
U u	rue	[y]	fuel, tuna
Y y [3]	yacht	[j]	yes, New York
Y y [4]	type	[i]	shorter than in feet

Consonants

Letter	French example	T&P phonetic alphabet	English example
B b	robe	[b]	baby, book
C c [5]	place	[s]	city, boss
C c [6]	canard	[k]	clock, kiss
Ç ç	leçon	[s]	city, boss
D d	disque	[d]	day, doctor
F f	femme	[f]	face, food
G g [7]	page	[ʒ]	forge, pleasure
G g [8]	gare	[g]	game, gold
H h	héros	[h]	silent [h]
J j	jour	[ʒ]	forge, pleasure
K k	kilo	[k]	clock, kiss
L l	aller	[l]	lace, people
M m	maison	[m]	magic, milk
N n	nom	[n]	name, normal
P p	papier	[p]	pencil, private
Q q	cinq	[k]	clock, kiss
R r	mars	[r]	rolled [r]
S s [9]	raison	[z]	zebra, please
S s [10]	sac	[s]	city, boss
T t	table	[t]	tourist, trip
V v	verre	[v]	very, river
W w	Taïwan	[w]	vase, winter

Letter	French example	T&P phonetic alphabet	English example
X x [11]	expliquer	[ks]	box, taxi
X x [12]	exact	[gz]	exam, exact
X x [13]	dix	[s]	city, boss
X x [14]	dixième	[z]	zebra, please
Z z	zéro	[z]	zebra, please

Combinations of letters

ai	faire	[ɛ]	man, bad
au	faute	[o], [oː]	floor, doctor
ay	payer	[eɪ]	age, today
ei	treize	[ɛ]	man, bad
eau	eau	[o], [oː]	floor, doctor
eu	beurre	[ø]	eternal, church
œ	œil	[ø]	eternal, church
œu	cœur	[øː]	first, thirsty
ou	nous	[u]	book
oi	noir	[wa]	watt, white
oy	voyage	[wa]	watt, white
qu	quartier	[k]	clock, kiss
ch	chat	[ʃ]	machine, shark
th	thé	[t]	tourist, trip
ph	photo	[f]	face, food
gu [15]	guerre	[g]	game, gold
ge [16]	géographie	[ʒ]	forge, pleasure
gn	ligne	[ɲ]	canyon, new
on, om	maison, nom	[ɔ̃]	strong

Comments

[1] before vowels
[2] elsewhere
[3] before vowels
[4] elsewhere
[5] before e, i, y
[6] elsewhere
[7] before e, i, y
[8] elsewhere
[9] between two vowels
[10] elsewhere
[11] most of cases
[12] rarely
[13] in dix, six, soixante

[14] in dixième, sixième
[15] before e, i, u
[16] before a, o, y

ABBREVIATIONS
used in the vocabulary

ab.	-	about
adj	-	adjective
adv	-	adverb
anim.	-	animate
as adj	-	attributive noun used as adjective
e.g.	-	for example
etc.	-	et cetera
fam.	-	familiar
fem.	-	feminine
form.	-	formal
inanim.	-	inanimate
masc.	-	masculine
math	-	mathematics
mil.	-	military
n	-	noun
pl	-	plural
pron.	-	pronoun
sb	-	somebody
sing.	-	singular
sth	-	something
v aux	-	auxiliary verb
vi	-	intransitive verb
vi, vt	-	intransitive, transitive verb
vt	-	transitive verb

m	-	masculine noun
f	-	feminine noun
m pl	-	masculine plural
f pl	-	feminine plural
m, f	-	masculine, feminine
conj	-	conjunction
prep	-	preposition
v imp	-	impersonnel verb
vp	-	pronominal verb

BASIC CONCEPTS

Basic concepts. Part 1

1. Pronouns

I, me	je	[ʒə]
you	tu	[ty]
he	il	[il]
she	elle	[ɛl]
it	ça	[sa]
we	nous	[nu]
you (to a group)	vous	[vu]
they (masc.)	ils	[il]
they (fem.)	elles	[ɛl]

2. Greetings. Salutations. Farewells

Hello! (fam.)	**Bonjour!**	[bɔ̃ʒur]
Hello! (form.)	**Bonjour!**	[bɔ̃ʒur]
Good morning!	**Bonjour!**	[bɔ̃ʒur]
Good afternoon!	**Bonjour!**	[bɔ̃ʒur]
Good evening!	**Bonsoir!**	[bɔ̃swar]
to say hello	**dire bonjour**	[dir bɔ̃ʒur]
Hi! (hello)	**Salut!**	[saly]
greeting (n)	**salut** (m)	[saly]
to greet (vt)	**saluer** (vt)	[salɥe]
How are you? (form.)	**Comment allez-vous?**	[kɔmɑ̃talevu]
How are you? (fam.)	**Comment ça va?**	[kɔmɑ̃ sa va]
What's new?	**Quoi de neuf?**	[kwa də nœf]
Bye-Bye! Goodbye!	**Au revoir!**	[orəvwar]
See you soon!	**À bientôt!**	[ɑ bjɛ̃to]
Farewell!	**Adieu!**	[adjø]
to say goodbye	**dire au revoir**	[dir ərəvwar]
So long!	**Salut!**	[saly]
Thank you!	**Merci!**	[mɛrsi]
Thank you very much!	**Merci beaucoup!**	[mɛrsi boku]
You're welcome	**Je vous en prie**	[ʒə vuzɑ̃pri]

Don't mention it!	Il n'y a pas de quoi	[il njapɑ də kwa]
It was nothing	Pas de quoi	[pɑ də kwa]
Excuse me! (fam.)	Excuse-moi!	[ɛkskyz mwa]
Excuse me! (form.)	Excusez-moi!	[ɛkskyze mwa]
to excuse (forgive)	excuser (vt)	[ɛkskyze]
to apologize (vi)	s'excuser (vp)	[sɛkskyze]
My apologies	Mes excuses	[me zɛkskyz]
I'm sorry!	Pardonnez-moi!	[pardɔne mwa]
to forgive (vt)	pardonner (vt)	[pardɔne]
It's okay!	C'est pas grave	[sepagrav]
please (adv)	s'il vous plaît	[silvuple]
Don't forget!	N'oubliez pas!	[nublije pɑ]
Certainly!	Bien sûr!	[bjɛ̃ sy:r]
Of course not!	Bien sûr que non!	[bjɛ̃ syr kə nɔ̃]
Okay! (I agree)	D'accord!	[dakɔr]
That's enough!	Ça suffit!	[sa syfi]

3. How to address

mister, sir	monsieur	[məsjø]
ma'am	madame	[madam]
miss	mademoiselle	[madmwazɛl]
young man	jeune homme	[ʒœn ɔm]
young man (little boy)	petit garçon	[pti garsɔ̃]
miss (little girl)	petite fille	[ptit fij]

4. Cardinal numbers. Part 1

0 zero	zéro	[zero]
1 one	un	[œ̃]
2 two	deux	[dø]
3 three	trois	[trwa]
4 four	quatre	[katr]
5 five	cinq	[sɛ̃k]
6 six	six	[sis]
7 seven	sept	[sɛt]
8 eight	huit	[ɥit]
9 nine	neuf	[nœf]
10 ten	dix	[dis]
11 eleven	onze	[ɔ̃z]
12 twelve	douze	[duz]
13 thirteen	treize	[trɛz]
14 fourteen	quatorze	[katɔrz]

15 fifteen	quinze	[kɛ̃z]
16 sixteen	seize	[sɛz]
17 seventeen	dix-sept	[disɛt]
18 eighteen	dix-huit	[dizyit]
19 nineteen	dix-neuf	[diznœf]
20 twenty	vingt	[vɛ̃]
21 twenty-one	vingt et un	[vɛ̃tœ̃]
22 twenty-two	vingt-deux	[vɛ̃tdø]
23 twenty-three	vingt-trois	[vɛ̃trwa]
30 thirty	trente	[trɑ̃t]
31 thirty-one	trente et un	[trɑ̃tœ̃]
32 thirty-two	trente-deux	[trɑ̃t dø]
33 thirty-three	trente-trois	[trɑ̃t trwa]
40 forty	quarante	[karɑ̃t]
41 forty-one	quarante et un	[karɑ̃tœ̃]
42 forty-two	quarante-deux	[karɑ̃t dø]
43 forty-three	quarante-trois	[karɑ̃t trwa]
50 fifty	cinquante	[sɛ̃kɑ̃t]
51 fifty-one	cinquante et un	[sɛ̃kɑ̃tœ̃]
52 fifty-two	cinquante-deux	[sɛ̃kɑ̃t dø]
53 fifty-three	cinquante-trois	[sɛ̃kɑ̃t trwa]
60 sixty	soixante	[swasɑ̃t]
61 sixty-one	soixante et un	[swasɑ̃tœ̃]
62 sixty-two	soixante-deux	[swasɑ̃t dø]
63 sixty-three	soixante-trois	[swasɑ̃t trwa]
70 seventy	soixante-dix	[swasɑ̃tdis]
71 seventy-one	soixante et onze	[swasɑ̃te ɔ̃z]
72 seventy-two	soixante-douze	[swasɑ̃t duz]
73 seventy-three	soixante-treize	[swasɑ̃t trɛz]
80 eighty	quatre-vingts	[katrəvɛ̃]
81 eighty-one	quatre-vingt et un	[katrəvɛ̃tœ̃]
82 eighty-two	quatre-vingt deux	[katrəvɛ̃ dø]
83 eighty-three	quatre-vingt trois	[katrəvɛ̃ trwa]
90 ninety	quatre-vingt-dix	[katrəvɛ̃dis]
91 ninety-one	quatre-vingt et onze	[katrəvɛ̃ teɔ̃z]
92 ninety-two	quatre-vingt-douze	[katrəvɛ̃ duz]
93 ninety-three	quatre-vingt-treize	[katrəvɛ̃ trɛz]

5. Cardinal numbers. Part 2

100 one hundred	cent	[sɑ̃]
200 two hundred	deux cents	[dø sɑ̃]

300 three hundred	trois cents	[trwa sɑ̃]
400 four hundred	quatre cents	[katr sɑ̃]
500 five hundred	cinq cents	[sɛ̆k sɑ̃]

600 six hundred	six cents	[si sɑ̃]
700 seven hundred	sept cents	[sɛt sɑ̃]
800 eight hundred	huit cents	[ɥi sɑ̃]
900 nine hundred	neuf cents	[nœf sɑ̃]

1000 one thousand	mille	[mil]
2000 two thousand	deux mille	[dø mil]
3000 three thousand	trois mille	[trwa mil]
10000 ten thousand	dix mille	[di mil]
one hundred thousand	cent mille	[sɑ̃ mil]
million	million (m)	[miljɔ̃]
billion	milliard (m)	[miljar]

6. Ordinal numbers

first (adj)	premier (adj)	[prəmje]
second (adj)	deuxième (adj)	[døzjɛm]
third (adj)	troisième (adj)	[trwazjɛm]
fourth (adj)	quatrième (adj)	[katrijɛm]
fifth (adj)	cinquième (adj)	[sɛ̆kjɛm]

sixth (adj)	sixième (adj)	[sizjɛm]
seventh (adj)	septième (adj)	[sɛtjɛm]
eighth (adj)	huitième (adj)	[ɥitjɛm]
ninth (adj)	neuvième (adj)	[nœvjɛm]
tenth (adj)	dixième (adj)	[dizjɛm]

7. Numbers. Fractions

fraction	fraction (f)	[fraksjɔ̃]
one half	un demi	[œ̃ dəmi]
one third	un tiers	[œ̃ tjɛr]
one quarter	un quart	[œ̃ kar]
one eighth	un huitième	[œn ɥitjɛm]
one tenth	un dixième	[œ̃ dizjɛm]
two thirds	deux tiers	[dø tjɛr]
three quarters	trois quarts	[trwa kar]

8. Numbers. Basic operations

| subtraction | soustraction (f) | [sustraksjɔ̃] |
| to subtract (vi, vt) | soustraire (vt) | [sustrɛr] |

division	division (f)	[divizjɔ̃]
to divide (vt)	diviser (vt)	[divize]
addition	addition (f)	[adisjɔ̃]
to add up (vt)	additionner (vt)	[adisjɔne]
to add (vi, vt)	ajouter (vt)	[aʒute]
multiplication	multiplication (f)	[myltiplikasjɔ̃]
to multiply (vt)	multiplier (vt)	[myltiplije]

9. Numbers. Miscellaneous

digit, figure	chiffre (m)	[ʃifr]
number	nombre (m)	[nɔ̃br]
numeral	adjectif (m) numéral	[adʒɛktif nymeral]
minus sign	moins (m)	[mwɛ̃]
plus sign	plus (m)	[ply]
formula	formule (f)	[fɔrmyl]
calculation	calcul (m)	[kalkyl]
to count (vt)	compter (vt)	[kɔ̃te]
to count up	calculer (vt)	[kalkyle]
to compare (vt)	comparer (vt)	[kɔ̃pare]
How much?	Combien?	[kɔ̃bjɛ̃]
sum, total	somme (f)	[sɔm]
result	résultat (m)	[rezylta]
remainder	reste (m)	[rɛst]
a few ...	quelques ...	[kɛlkə]
few, little (adv)	peu de ...	[pø də]
the rest	reste (m)	[rɛst]
one and a half	un et demi	[œne dəmi]
dozen	douzaine (f)	[duzɛn]
in half (adv)	en deux	[ɑ̃ dø]
equally (evenly)	en parties égales	[ɑ̃ parti egal]
half	moitié (f)	[mwatje]
time (three ~s)	fois (f)	[fwa]

10. The most important verbs. Part 1

to advise (vt)	conseiller (vt)	[kɔ̃seje]
to agree (say yes)	être d'accord	[ɛtr dakɔr]
to answer (vi, vt)	répondre (vi, vt)	[repɔ̃dr]
to apologize (vi)	s'excuser (vp)	[sɛkskyze]
to arrive (vi)	venir (vi)	[vənir]
to ask (~ oneself)	demander (vt)	[dəmɑ̃de]
to ask (~ sb to do sth)	demander (vt)	[dəmɑ̃de]

to be (vi)	être (vi)	[ɛtr]
to be afraid	avoir peur	[avwar pœr]
to be hungry	avoir faim	[avwar fɛ̃]
to be interested in …	s'intéresser (vp)	[sɛ̃terese]
to be needed	être nécessaire	[ɛtr nesesɛr]
to be surprised	s'étonner (vp)	[setɔne]
to be thirsty	avoir soif	[avwar swaf]
to begin (vt)	commencer (vt)	[kɔmɑ̃se]
to belong to …	appartenir à …	[apartənir a]
to boast (vi)	se vanter (vp)	[sə vɑ̃te]
to break (split into pieces)	casser (vt)	[kase]
to call (for help)	appeler (vt)	[aple]
can (v aux)	pouvoir (v aux)	[puvwar]
to catch (vt)	attraper (vt)	[atrape]
to change (vt)	changer (vt)	[ʃɑ̃ʒe]
to choose (select)	choisir (vt)	[ʃwazir]
to come down	descendre (vi)	[desɑ̃dr]
to come in (enter)	entrer (vi)	[ɑ̃tre]
to compare (vt)	comparer (vt)	[kɔ̃pare]
to complain (vi, vt)	se plaindre (vp)	[sə plɛ̃dr]
to confuse (mix up)	confondre (vt)	[kɔ̃fɔ̃dr]
to continue (vt)	continuer (vt)	[kɔ̃tinɥe]
to control (vt)	contrôler (vt)	[kɔ̃trole]
to cook (dinner)	préparer (vt)	[prepare]
to cost (vt)	coûter (vt)	[kute]
to count (add up)	compter (vi, vt)	[kɔ̃te]
to count on …	compter sur …	[kɔ̃te syr]
to create (vt)	créer (vt)	[kree]
to cry (weep)	pleurer (vi)	[plœre]

11. The most important verbs. Part 2

to deceive (vi, vt)	tromper (vt)	[trɔ̃pe]
to decorate (tree, street)	décorer (vt)	[dekɔre]
to defend (a country, etc.)	défendre (vt)	[defɑ̃dr]
to demand (request firmly)	exiger (vt)	[ɛgziʒe]
to dig (vt)	creuser (vt)	[krøze]
to discuss (vt)	discuter (vt)	[diskyte]
to do (vt)	faire (vt)	[fɛr]
to doubt (have doubts)	douter (vt)	[dute]
to drop (let fall)	faire tomber	[fɛr tɔ̃be]
to excuse (forgive)	excuser (vt)	[ɛkskyze]
to exist (vi)	exister (vi)	[ɛgziste]

to expect (foresee)	**prévoir** (vt)	[prevwar]
to explain (vt)	**expliquer** (vt)	[ɛksplike]
to fall (vi)	**tomber** (vi)	[tõbe]
to find (vt)	**trouver** (vt)	[truve]
to finish (vt)	**finir** (vt)	[finir]
to fly (vi)	**voler** (vi)	[vɔle]
to follow ... (come after)	**suivre** (vt)	[sɥivr]
to forget (vi, vt)	**oublier** (vt)	[ublije]
to forgive (vt)	**pardonner** (vt)	[pardɔne]
to give (vt)	**donner** (vt)	[dɔne]
to give a hint	**donner un indice**	[dɔne ynɛ̃dis]
to go (on foot)	**aller** (vi)	[ale]
to go for a swim	**se baigner** (vp)	[sə beɲe]
to go out (from ...)	**sortir** (vi)	[sɔrtir]
to guess right	**deviner** (vt)	[dəvine]
to have (vt)	**avoir** (vt)	[avwar]
to have breakfast	**prendre le petit déjeuner**	[prãdr ləpti deʒœne]
to have dinner	**dîner** (vi)	[dine]
to have lunch	**déjeuner** (vi)	[deʒœne]
to hear (vt)	**entendre** (vt)	[ãtãdr]
to help (vt)	**aider** (vt)	[ede]
to hide (vt)	**cacher** (vt)	[kaʃe]
to hope (vi, vt)	**espérer** (vi)	[ɛspere]
to hunt (vi, vt)	**chasser** (vi, vt)	[ʃase]
to hurry (vi)	**être pressé**	[ɛtr prese]

12. The most important verbs. Part 3

to inform (vt)	**informer** (vt)	[ɛ̃fɔrme]
to insist (vi, vt)	**insister** (vi)	[ɛ̃siste]
to insult (vt)	**insulter** (vt)	[ɛ̃sylte]
to invite (vt)	**inviter** (vt)	[ɛ̃vite]
to joke (vi)	**plaisanter** (vi)	[plɛzãte]
to keep (vt)	**garder** (vt)	[garde]
to keep silent	**rester silencieux**	[rɛste silãsjø]
to kill (vt)	**tuer** (vt)	[tɥe]
to know (sb)	**connaître** (vt)	[kɔnɛtr]
to know (sth)	**savoir** (vt)	[savwar]
to laugh (vi)	**rire** (vi)	[rir]
to liberate (city, etc.)	**libérer** (vt)	[libere]
to like (I like ...)	**plaire** (vt)	[plɛr]
to look for ... (search)	**chercher** (vt)	[ʃɛrʃe]
to love (sb)	**aimer** (vt)	[eme]

to make a mistake	se tromper (vp)	[sə trɔ̃pe]
to manage, to run	diriger (vt)	[diriʒe]
to mean (signify)	signifier (vt)	[siɲifje]
to mention (talk about)	mentionner (vt)	[mɑ̃sjɔne]
to miss (school, etc.)	manquer (vt)	[mɑ̃ke]
to notice (see)	apercevoir (vt)	[apɛrsəvwar]
to object (vi, vt)	objecter (vt)	[ɔbʒɛkte]
to observe (see)	observer (vt)	[ɔpsɛrve]
to open (vt)	ouvrir (vt)	[uvrir]
to order (meal, etc.)	commander (vt)	[kɔmɑ̃de]
to order (mil.)	ordonner (vt)	[ɔrdɔne]
to own (possess)	posséder (vt)	[pɔsede]
to participate (vi)	participer à ...	[partisipe a]
to pay (vi, vt)	payer (vi, vt)	[peje]
to permit (vt)	permettre (vt)	[pɛrmɛtr]
to plan (vt)	planifier (vt)	[planifje]
to play (children)	jouer (vt)	[ʒwe]
to pray (vi, vt)	prier (vt)	[prije]
to prefer (vt)	préférer (vt)	[prefere]
to promise (vt)	promettre (vt)	[prɔmɛtr]
to pronounce (vt)	prononcer (vt)	[prɔnɔ̃se]
to propose (vt)	proposer (vt)	[prɔpoze]
to punish (vt)	punir (vt)	[pynir]
to read (vi, vt)	lire (vi, vt)	[lir]
to recommend (vt)	recommander (vt)	[rəkɔmɑ̃de]
to refuse (vi, vt)	se refuser (vp)	[sə rəfyze]
to regret (be sorry)	regretter (vt)	[rəgrɛte]
to rent (sth from sb)	louer (vt)	[lwe]
to repeat (say again)	répéter (vt)	[repete]
to reserve, to book	réserver (vt)	[rezɛrve]
to run (vi)	courir (vt)	[kurir]

13. The most important verbs. Part 4

to save (rescue)	sauver (vt)	[sove]
to say (~ thank you)	dire (vt)	[dir]
to scold (vt)	gronder (vt)	[grɔ̃de]
to see (vt)	voir (vt)	[vwar]
to sell (vt)	vendre (vt)	[vɑ̃dr]
to send (vt)	envoyer (vt)	[ɑ̃vwaje]
to shoot (vi)	tirer (vi)	[tire]
to shout (vi)	crier (vi)	[krije]
to show (vt)	montrer (vt)	[mɔ̃tre]
to sign (document)	signer (vt)	[siɲe]

to sit down (vi)	**s'asseoir** (vp)	[saswar]
to smile (vi)	**sourire** (vi)	[surir]
to speak (vi, vt)	**parler** (vi, vt)	[parle]
to steal (money, etc.)	**voler** (vt)	[vɔle]
to stop (please ~ calling me)	**cesser** (vt)	[sese]
to stop (for pause, etc.)	**s'arrêter** (vp)	[sarete]
to study (vt)	**étudier** (vt)	[etydje]
to swim (vi)	**nager** (vi)	[naʒe]
to take (vt)	**prendre** (vt)	[prɑ̃dr]
to think (vi, vt)	**penser** (vi, vt)	[pɑ̃se]
to threaten (vt)	**menacer** (vt)	[mənase]
to touch (with hands)	**toucher** (vt)	[tuʃe]
to translate (vt)	**traduire** (vt)	[tradɥir]
to trust (vt)	**avoir confiance**	[avwar kɔ̃fjɑ̃s]
to try (attempt)	**essayer** (vt)	[eseje]
to turn (~ to the left)	**tourner** (vi)	[turne]
to underestimate (vt)	**sous-estimer** (vt)	[suzɛstime]
to understand (vt)	**comprendre** (vt)	[kɔ̃prɑ̃dr]
to unite (vt)	**réunir** (vt)	[reynir]
to wait (vt)	**attendre** (vt)	[atɑ̃dr]
to want (wish, desire)	**vouloir** (vt)	[vulwar]
to warn (vt)	**avertir** (vt)	[avɛrtir]
to work (vi)	**travailler** (vi)	[travaje]
to write (vt)	**écrire** (vt)	[ekrir]
to write down	**prendre en note**	[prɑ̃dr ɑ̃ nɔt]

14. Colors

color	**couleur** (f)	[kulœr]
shade (tint)	**teinte** (f)	[tɛ̃t]
hue	**ton** (m)	[tɔ̃]
rainbow	**arc-en-ciel** (m)	[arkɑ̃sjɛl]
white (adj)	**blanc** (adj)	[blɑ̃]
black (adj)	**noir** (adj)	[nwar]
gray (adj)	**gris** (adj)	[gri]
green (adj)	**vert** (adj)	[vɛr]
yellow (adj)	**jaune** (adj)	[ʒon]
red (adj)	**rouge** (adj)	[ruʒ]
blue (adj)	**bleu** (adj)	[blø]
light blue (adj)	**bleu clair** (adj)	[blø klɛr]
pink (adj)	**rose** (adj)	[roz]
orange (adj)	**orange** (adj)	[ɔrɑ̃ʒ]

violet (adj)	**violet** (adj)	[vjɔlɛ]
brown (adj)	**brun** (adj)	[brœ̃]
golden (adj)	**d'or** (adj)	[dɔr]
silvery (adj)	**argenté** (adj)	[arʒɑ̃te]
beige (adj)	**beige** (adj)	[bɛʒ]
cream (adj)	**crème** (adj)	[krɛm]
turquoise (adj)	**turquoise** (adj)	[tyrkwaz]
cherry red (adj)	**rouge cerise** (adj)	[ruʒ səriz]
lilac (adj)	**lilas** (adj)	[lila]
crimson (adj)	**framboise** (adj)	[frɑ̃bwaz]
light (adj)	**clair** (adj)	[klɛr]
dark (adj)	**foncé** (adj)	[fɔ̃se]
bright, vivid (adj)	**vif** (adj)	[vif]
colored (pencils)	**de couleur** (adj)	[də kulœr]
color (e.g., ~ film)	**en couleurs** (adj)	[ɑ̃ kulœr]
black-and-white (adj)	**noir et blanc** (adj)	[nwar e blɑ̃]
plain (one-colored)	**monochrome** (adj)	[mɔnɔkrom]
multicolored (adj)	**multicolore** (adj)	[myltikɔlɔr]

15. Questions

Who?	**Qui?**	[ki]
What?	**Quoi?**	[kwa]
Where? (at, in)	**Où?**	[u]
Where (to)?	**Où?**	[u]
From where?	**D'où?**	[du]
When?	**Quand?**	[kɑ̃]
Why? (What for?)	**Pourquoi?**	[purkwa]
Why? (reason)	**Pourquoi?**	[purkwa]
What for?	**À quoi bon?**	[ɑ kwa bɔ̃]
How? (in what way)	**Comment?**	[kɔmɑ̃]
What? (What kind of ...?)	**Quel?**	[kɛl]
Which?	**Lequel?**	[ləkɛl]
To whom?	**À qui?**	[ɑ ki]
About whom?	**De qui?**	[də ki]
About what?	**De quoi?**	[də kwa]
With whom?	**Avec qui?**	[avɛk ki]
How many? How much?	**Combien?**	[kɔ̃bjɛ̃]
Whose?	**À qui?**	[ɑ ki]

16. Prepositions

with (accompanied by)	**avec** ... (prep)	[avɛk]
without	**sans** ... (prep)	[sɑ̃]
to (indicating direction)	**à** ... (prep)	[ɑ]
about (talking ~ ...)	**de** ... (prep)	[də]
before (in time)	**avant** (prep)	[avɑ̃]
in front of ...	**devant** (prep)	[dəvɑ̃]
under (beneath, below)	**sous** ... (prep)	[su]
above (over)	**au-dessus de** ... (prep)	[odsy də]
on (atop)	**sur** ... (prep)	[syr]
from (off, out of)	**de** ... (prep)	[də]
of (made from)	**en** ... (prep)	[ɑ̃]
in (e.g., ~ ten minutes)	**dans** ... (prep)	[dɑ̃]
over (across the top of)	**par dessus** ... (prep)	[par dəsy]

17. Function words. Adverbs. Part 1

Where? (at, in)	**Où?**	[u]
here (adv)	**ici** (adv)	[isi]
there (adv)	**là-bas** (adv)	[laba]
somewhere (to be)	**quelque part** (adv)	[kɛlkə par]
nowhere (not anywhere)	**nulle part** (adv)	[nyl par]
by (near, beside)	**près de** ... (prep)	[prɛ də]
by the window	**près de la fenêtre**	[prɛdə la fənɛtr]
Where (to)?	**Où?**	[u]
here (e.g., come ~!)	**ici** (adv)	[isi]
there (e.g., to go ~)	**là-bas** (adv)	[laba]
from here (adv)	**d'ici** (adv)	[disi]
from there (adv)	**de là-bas** (adv)	[də laba]
close (adv)	**près** (adv)	[prɛ]
far (adv)	**loin** (adv)	[lwɛ̃]
near (e.g., ~ Paris)	**près de** ...	[prɛ də]
nearby (adv)	**tout près** (adv)	[tu prɛ]
not far (adv)	**pas loin** (adv)	[pɑ lwɛ̃]
left (adj)	**gauche** (adj)	[goʃ]
on the left	**à gauche** (adv)	[agoʃ]
to the left	**à gauche** (adv)	[agoʃ]
right (adj)	**droit** (adj)	[drwa]
on the right	**à droite** (adv)	[adrwat]

to the right	à droite (adv)	[adrwat]
in front (adv)	devant (adv)	[dəvã]
front (as adj)	de devant (adj)	[də dəvã]
ahead (look ~)	en avant (adv)	[ɑn avã]
behind (adv)	derrière (adv)	[dɛrjɛr]
from behind	par derrière (adv)	[par dɛrjɛr]
back (towards the rear)	en arrière (adv)	[ɑn arjɛr]
middle	milieu (m)	[miljø]
in the middle	au milieu (adv)	[omiljø]
at the side	de côté (adv)	[də kote]
everywhere (adv)	partout (adv)	[partu]
around (in all directions)	autour (adv)	[otur]
from inside	de l'intérieur	[də lɛ̃terjœr]
somewhere (to go)	quelque part (adv)	[kɛlkə par]
straight (directly)	tout droit (adv)	[tu drwa]
back (e.g., come ~)	en arrière (adv)	[ɑn arjɛr]
from anywhere	de quelque part	[də kɛlkə par]
from somewhere	de quelque part	[də kɛlkə par]
firstly (adv)	premièrement (adv)	[prəmjɛrmã]
secondly (adv)	deuxièmement (adv)	[døzjɛmmã]
thirdly (adv)	troisièmement (adv)	[trwazjɛmmã]
suddenly (adv)	soudain (adv)	[sudɛ̃]
at first (adv)	au début (adv)	[odeby]
for the first time	pour la première fois	[pur la prəmjɛr fwa]
long before ...	bien avant ...	[bjɛn avã]
anew (over again)	de nouveau (adv)	[də nuvo]
for good (adv)	pour toujours (adv)	[pur tuʒur]
never (adv)	jamais (adv)	[ʒamɛ]
again (adv)	encore (adv)	[ãkɔr]
now (adv)	maintenant (adv)	[mɛ̃tnã]
often (adv)	souvent (adv)	[suvã]
then (adv)	alors (adv)	[alɔr]
urgently (quickly)	d'urgence (adv)	[dyrʒãs]
usually (adv)	d'habitude (adv)	[dabityd]
by the way, ...	à propos, ...	[aprɔpo]
possible (that is ~)	c'est possible	[sepɔsibl]
probably (adv)	probablement (adv)	[prɔbabləmã]
maybe (adv)	peut-être (adv)	[pøtɛtr]
besides ...	en plus, ...	[ãplys]
that's why ...	c'est pourquoi ...	[se purkwa]
in spite of ...	malgré ...	[malgre]
thanks to ...	grâce à ...	[gras a]
what (pron.)	quoi (pron.)	[kwa]

that (conj.)	que (conj)	[kə]
something	quelque chose (pron.)	[kɛlkə ʃoz]
anything (something)	quelque chose (pron.)	[kɛlkə ʃoz]
nothing	rien	[rjɛ̃]

who (pron.)	qui (pron.)	[ki]
someone	quelqu'un (pron.)	[kɛlkœ̃]
somebody	quelqu'un (pron.)	[kɛlkœ̃]

nobody	personne (pron.)	[pɛrsɔn]
nowhere (a voyage to ~)	nulle part (adv)	[nyl par]
nobody's	de personne	[də pɛrsɔn]
somebody's	de n'importe qui	[də nɛ̃pɔrt ki]

so (I'm ~ glad)	comme ça (adv)	[kɔmsa]
also (as well)	également (adv)	[egalmɑ̃]
too (as well)	aussi (adv)	[osi]

18. Function words. Adverbs. Part 2

Why?	Pourquoi?	[purkwa]
for some reason	on ne sait pourquoi	[ɔ̃nə sɛ purkwa]
because ...	parce que ...	[parskə]
for some purpose	pour une raison quelconque	[pur yn rɛzɔ̃ kɛlkɔ̃k]

and	et (conj)	[e]
or	ou (conj)	[u]
but	mais (conj)	[mɛ]
for (e.g., ~ me)	pour ... (prep)	[pur]

too (~ many people)	trop (adv)	[tro]
only (exclusively)	seulement (adv)	[sœlmɑ̃]
exactly (adv)	précisément (adv)	[presizemɑ̃]
about (more or less)	autour de ... (prep)	[otur də]

approximately (adv)	approximativement	[aprɔksimativmɑ̃]
approximate (adj)	approximatif (adj)	[aprɔksimatif]
almost (adv)	presque (adv)	[prɛsk]
the rest	reste (m)	[rɛst]

the other (second)	l'autre (adj)	[lotr]
other (different)	autre (adj)	[otr]
each (adj)	chaque (adj)	[ʃak]
any (no matter which)	n'importe quel (adj)	[nɛ̃pɔrt kɛl]
many, much (a lot of)	beaucoup (adv)	[boku]
many people	plusieurs (pron.)	[plyzjœr]
all (everyone)	touts les ... , toutes les ...	[tut le], [tut le]
in return for ...	en échange de ...	[ɑn eʃɑ̃ʒ də ...]

in exchange (adv)	**en échange** (adv)	[ɑn eʃɑ̃ʒ]
by hand (made)	**à la main** (adv)	[ɑlamɛ̃]
hardly (negative opinion)	**peu probable** (adj)	[pø prɔbabl]
probably (adv)	**probablement** (adv)	[prɔbabləmɑ̃]
on purpose (adv)	**exprès** (adv)	[ɛksprɛ]
by accident (adv)	**par hasard** (adv)	[par azar]
very (adv)	**très** (adv)	[trɛ]
for example (adv)	**par exemple** (adv)	[par ɛgzɑ̃p]
between	**entre ...** (prep)	[ɑ̃tr]
among	**parmi ...** (prep)	[parmi]
so much (such a lot)	**autant** (adv)	[otɑ̃]
especially (adv)	**surtout** (adv)	[syrtu]

Basic concepts. Part 2

19. Weekdays

Monday	**lundi** (m)	[lœ̃di]
Tuesday	**mardi** (m)	[mardi]
Wednesday	**mercredi** (m)	[mɛrkrədi]
Thursday	**jeudi** (m)	[ʒødi]
Friday	**vendredi** (m)	[vɑ̃drədi]
Saturday	**samedi** (m)	[samdi]
Sunday	**dimanche** (m)	[dimɑ̃ʃ]
today (adv)	**aujourd'hui** (adv)	[oʒurdɥi]
tomorrow (adv)	**demain** (adv)	[dəmɛ̃]
the day after tomorrow	**après-demain** (adv)	[aprɛdmɛ̃]
yesterday (adv)	**hier** (adv)	[ijɛr]
the day before yesterday	**avant-hier** (adv)	[avɑ̃tjɛr]
day	**jour** (m)	[ʒur]
working day	**jour** (m) **ouvrable**	[ʒur uvrabl]
public holiday	**jour** (m) **férié**	[ʒur ferje]
day off	**jour** (m) **de repos**	[ʒur də rəpo]
weekend	**week-end** (m)	[wikɛnd]
all day long	**toute la journée**	[tut la ʒurne]
next day (adv)	**le lendemain**	[lɑ̃dmɛ̃]
two days ago	**il y a 2 jours**	[ilja də ʒur]
the day before	**la veille**	[la vɛj]
daily (adj)	**quotidien** (adj)	[kɔtidjɛ̃]
every day (adv)	**tous les jours**	[tu le ʒur]
week	**semaine** (f)	[səmɛn]
last week (adv)	**la semaine dernière**	[la səmɛn dɛrnjɛr]
next week (adv)	**la semaine prochaine**	[la səmɛn prɔʃɛn]
weekly (adj)	**hebdomadaire** (adj)	[ɛbdɔmadɛr]
every week (adv)	**chaque semaine**	[ʃak səmɛn]
twice a week	**2 fois par semaine**	[dø fwa par səmɛn]
every Tuesday	**tous les mardis**	[tu le mardi]

20. Hours. Day and night

morning	**matin** (m)	[matɛ̃]
in the morning	**le matin**	[lə matɛ̃]
noon, midday	**midi** (m)	[midi]

in the afternoon	dans l'après-midi	[dɑ̃ laprɛmidi]
evening	soir (m)	[swar]
in the evening	le soir	[lə swar]
night	nuit (f)	[nɥi]
at night	la nuit	[la nɥi]
midnight	minuit (f)	[minɥi]
second	seconde (f)	[səgɔ̃d]
minute	minute (f)	[minyt]
hour	heure (f)	[œr]
half an hour	demi-heure (f)	[dəmijœr]
quarter of an hour	un quart d'heure	[œ̃ kar dœr]
fifteen minutes	quinze minutes	[kɛ̃z minyt]
24 hours	vingt-quatre heures	[vɛ̃tkatr œr]
sunrise	lever (m) du soleil	[ləve dy sɔlɛj]
dawn	aube (f)	[ob]
early morning	pointe (f) du jour	[pwɛ̃t dy ʒur]
sunset	coucher (m) du soleil	[kuʃe dy sɔlɛj]
early in the morning	tôt le matin	[to lə matɛ̃]
this morning	ce matin	[sə matɛ̃]
tomorrow morning	demain matin	[dəmɛ̃ matɛ̃]
this afternoon	cet après-midi	[sɛt aprɛmidi]
in the afternoon	dans l'après-midi	[dɑ̃ laprɛmidi]
tomorrow afternoon	demain après-midi	[dəmɛn aprɛmidi]
tonight (this evening)	ce soir	[sə swar]
tomorrow night	demain soir	[dəmɛ̃ swar]
at 3 o'clock sharp	à 3 heures précises	[ɑ trwa zœr presiz]
about 4 o'clock	autour de 4 heures	[otur də katr œr]
by 12 o'clock	vers midi	[vɛr midi]
in 20 minutes	dans 20 minutes	[dɑ̃ vɛ̃ minyt]
in an hour	dans une heure	[dɑ̃zyn œr]
on time (adv)	à temps	[ɑ tɑ̃]
a quarter of ...	moins le quart	[mwɛ̃ lə kar]
within an hour	en une heure	[ɑnyn œr]
every 15 minutes	tous les quarts d'heure	[tu le kar dœr]
round the clock	24 heures sur 24	[vɛ̃tkatr œr syr vɛ̃tkatr]

21. Months. Seasons

January	janvier (m)	[ʒɑ̃vje]
February	février (m)	[fevrije]
March	mars (m)	[mars]
April	avril (m)	[avril]

| May | mai (m) | [mɛ] |
| June | juin (m) | [ʒɥɛ̃] |

July	juillet (m)	[ʒɥijɛ]
August	août (m)	[ut]
September	septembre (m)	[sɛparemɑ̃]
October	octobre (m)	[ɔktɔbr]
November	novembre (m)	[nɔvɑ̃br]
December	décembre (m)	[desɑ̃br]

spring	printemps (m)	[prɛ̃tɑ̃]
in spring	au printemps	[oprɛ̃tɑ̃]
spring (as adj)	de printemps (adj)	[də prɛ̃tɑ̃]

summer	été (m)	[ete]
in summer	en été	[ɑn ete]
summer (as adj)	d'été (adj)	[dete]

fall	automne (m)	[otɔn]
in fall	en automne	[ɑn otɔn]
fall (as adj)	d'automne (adj)	[dotɔn]

winter	hiver (m)	[ivɛr]
in winter	en hiver	[ɑn ivɛr]
winter (as adj)	d'hiver (adj)	[divɛr]

month	mois (m)	[mwa]
this month	ce mois	[sə mwa]
next month	le mois prochain	[lə mwa prɔʃɛ̃]
last month	le mois dernier	[lə mwa dɛrnje]

a month ago	il y a un mois	[ilja œ̃ mwa]
in a month	dans un mois	[dɑ̃zœn mwa]
in two months	dans 2 mois	[dɑ̃ dø mwa]
the whole month	tout le mois	[tu lə mwa]
all month long	tout un mois	[tutœ̃ mwa]

monthly (~ magazine)	mensuel (adj)	[mɑ̃sɥɛl]
monthly (adv)	tous les mois	[tu le mwa]
every month	chaque mois	[ʃak mwa]
twice a month	2 fois par mois	[dø fwa par mwa]

year	année (f)	[ane]
this year	cette année	[sɛt ane]
next year	l'année prochaine	[lane prɔʃɛn]
last year	l'année dernière	[lane dɛrnjɛr]

a year ago	il y a un an	[ilja œnɑ̃]
in a year	dans un an	[dɑ̃zœn ɑ̃]
in two years	dans 2 ans	[dɑ̃ dø zɑ̃]
the whole year	toute l'année	[tut lane]
all year long	toute une année	[tutyn ane]

every year	chaque année	[ʃak ane]
annual (adj)	annuel (adj)	[anɥɛl]
annually (adv)	tous les ans	[tu lezɑ̃]
4 times a year	4 fois par an	[katr fwa parɑ̃]

date (e.g., today's ~)	date (f)	[dat]
date (e.g., ~ of birth)	date (f)	[dat]
calendar	calendrier (m)	[kalɑ̃drije]

half a year	six mois	[si mwa]
six months	semestre (m)	[səmɛstr]
season (summer, etc.)	saison (f)	[sɛzɔ̃]
century	siècle (m)	[sjɛkl]

22. Units of measurement

weight	poids (m)	[pwa]
length	longueur (f)	[lɔ̃gœr]
width	largeur (f)	[larʒœr]
height	hauteur (f)	[otœr]
depth	profondeur (f)	[prɔfɔ̃dœr]
volume	volume (m)	[vɔlym]
area	surface (f)	[syrfas]

gram	gramme (m)	[gram]
milligram	milligramme (m)	[miligram]
kilogram	kilogramme (m)	[kilɔgram]
ton	tonne (f)	[tɔn]
pound	livre (f)	[livr]
ounce	once (f)	[ɔ̃s]

meter	mètre (m)	[mɛtr]
millimeter	millimètre (m)	[milimɛtr]
centimeter	centimètre (m)	[sɑ̃timɛtr]
kilometer	kilomètre (m)	[kilɔmɛtr]
mile	mille (m)	[mil]

inch	pouce (m)	[pus]
foot	pied (m)	[pje]
yard	yard (m)	[jard]

square meter	mètre (m) carré	[mɛtr kare]
hectare	hectare (m)	[ɛktar]

liter	litre (m)	[litr]
degree	degré (m)	[dəgre]
volt	volt (m)	[vɔlt]
ampere	ampère (m)	[ɑ̃pɛr]
horsepower	cheval-vapeur (m)	[ʃəvalvapœr]
quantity	quantité (f)	[kɑ̃tite]

a little bit of ...	un peu de ...	[œ̃ pø də]
half	moitié (f)	[mwatje]
dozen	douzaine (f)	[duzɛn]
piece (item)	pièce (f)	[pjɛs]

| size | dimension (f) | [dimɑ̃sjɔ̃] |
| scale (map ~) | échelle (f) | [eʃɛl] |

minimal (adj)	minimal (adj)	[minimal]
the smallest (adj)	le plus petit (adj)	[lə ply pəti]
medium (adj)	moyen (adj)	[mwajɛ̃]
maximal (adj)	maximal (adj)	[maksimal]
the largest (adj)	le plus grand (adj)	[lə ply grɑ̃]

23. Containers

jar (glass)	bocal (m)	[bɔkal]
can	boîte (f) en fer-blanc	[bwat ɑ̃ fɛrblɑ̃]
bucket	seau (m)	[so]
barrel	tonneau (m)	[tɔno]

basin (for washing)	bassine (f)	[basin]
tank (for liquid, gas)	réservoir (m)	[rezɛrvwar]
hip flask	flasque (f)	[flask]
jerrycan	jerrycan (m)	[ʒerikan]
cistern (tank)	citerne (f)	[sitɛrn]

mug	grande tasse (f)	[grɑ̃d tɑs]
cup (of coffee, etc.)	tasse (f)	[tɑs]
saucer	soucoupe (f)	[sukup]
glass (tumbler)	verre (m)	[vɛr]
wineglass	verre (m) à pied	[vɛr a pje]
saucepan	casserole (f)	[kasrɔl]

| bottle (~ of wine) | bouteille (f) | [butɛj] |
| neck (of the bottle) | goulot (m) | [gulo] |

carafe	carafe (f)	[karaf]
pitcher (earthenware)	cruche (f)	[kryʃ]
vessel (container)	récipient (m)	[resipjɑ̃]
pot (crock)	pot (m)	[po]
vase	vase (m)	[vaz]

bottle (~ of perfume)	flacon (m)	[flakɔ̃]
vial, small bottle	fiole (f)	[fjɔl]
tube (of toothpaste)	tube (m)	[tyb]

sack (bag)	sac (m)	[sak]
bag (paper ~, plastic ~)	sac (m)	[sak]
pack (of cigarettes, etc.)	paquet (m)	[pakɛ]

box (e.g., shoebox)	**boîte** (f)	[bwat]
crate	**caisse** (f)	[kɛs]
basket	**panier** (m)	[panje]

HUMAN BEING

Human being. The body

24. Head

head	tête (f)	[tɛt]
face	visage (m)	[vizaʒ]
nose	nez (m)	[ne]
mouth	bouche (f)	[buʃ]

eye	œil (m)	[œj]
eyes	les yeux	[lezjø]
pupil	pupille (f)	[pypij]
eyebrow	sourcil (m)	[sursi]
eyelash	cil (m)	[sil]
eyelid	paupière (f)	[popjɛr]

tongue	langue (f)	[lɑ̃g]
tooth	dent (f)	[dɑ̃]
lips	lèvres (f pl)	[lɛvr]
cheekbones	pommettes (f pl)	[pomɛt]
gum	gencive (f)	[ʒɑ̃siv]
palate	palais (m)	[palɛ]

nostrils	narines (f pl)	[narin]
chin	menton (m)	[mɑ̃tɔ̃]
jaw	mâchoire (f)	[mɑʃwar]
cheek	joue (f)	[ʒu]

forehead	front (m)	[frɔ̃]
temple	tempe (f)	[tɑ̃p]
ear	oreille (f)	[ɔrɛj]
back of the head	nuque (f)	[nyk]
neck	cou (m)	[ku]
throat	gorge (f)	[gɔrʒ]

hair	cheveux (m pl)	[ʃəvø]
hairstyle	coiffure (f)	[kwafyr]
haircut	coupe (f)	[kup]
wig	perruque (f)	[peryk]

mustache	moustache (f)	[mustaʃ]
beard	barbe (f)	[barb]
to have (a beard, etc.)	porter (vt)	[pɔrte]

| braid | tresse (f) | [trɛs] |
| sideburns | favoris (m pl) | [favɔri] |

red-haired (adj)	roux (adj)	[ru]
gray (hair)	gris (adj)	[gri]
bald (adj)	chauve (adj)	[ʃov]
bald patch	calvitie (f)	[kalvisi]

| ponytail | queue (f) de cheval | [kø də ʃəval] |
| bangs | frange (f) | [frɑ̃ʒ] |

25. Human body

| hand | main (f) | [mɛ̃] |
| arm | bras (m) | [bra] |

finger	doigt (m)	[dwa]
toe	orteil (m)	[ɔrtɛj]
thumb	pouce (m)	[pus]
little finger	petit doigt (m)	[pəti dwa]
nail	ongle (m)	[ɔ̃gl]

fist	poing (m)	[pwɛ̃]
palm	paume (f)	[pom]
wrist	poignet (m)	[pwaɲɛ]
forearm	avant-bras (m)	[avɑ̃bra]
elbow	coude (m)	[kud]
shoulder	épaule (f)	[epol]

leg	jambe (f)	[ʒɑ̃b]
foot	pied (m)	[pje]
knee	genou (m)	[ʒənu]
calf (part of leg)	mollet (m)	[mɔlɛ]
hip	hanche (f)	[ɑ̃ʃ]
heel	talon (m)	[talɔ̃]

body	corps (m)	[kɔr]
stomach	ventre (m)	[vɑ̃tr]
chest	poitrine (f)	[pwatrin]
breast	sein (m)	[sɛ̃]
flank	côté (m)	[kote]
back	dos (m)	[do]
lower back	reins (m pl)	[rɛ̃]
waist	taille (f)	[taj]

navel	nombril (m)	[nɔ̃bril]
buttocks	fesses (f pl)	[fɛs]
bottom	derrière (m)	[dɛrjɛr]
beauty mark	grain (m) de beauté	[grɛ̃ də bote]
birthmark	tache (f) de vin	[taʃ də vɛ̃]

tattoo	**tatouage** (m)	[tatwaʒ]
scar	**cicatrice** (f)	[sikatris]

Clothing & Accessories

26. Outerwear. Coats

clothes	**vêtement** (m)	[vɛtmɑ̃]
outer clothes	**survêtement** (m)	[syrvɛtmɑ̃]
winter clothes	**vêtement** (m) **d'hiver**	[vɛtmɑ̃ divɛr]
overcoat	**manteau** (m)	[mɑ̃to]
fur coat	**manteau** (m) **de fourrure**	[mɑ̃to də furyr]
fur jacket	**veste** (f) **en fourrure**	[vɛst ɑ̃ furyr]
down coat	**manteau** (m) **de duvet**	[manto də dyvɛ]
jacket (e.g., leather ~)	**veste** (f)	[vɛst]
raincoat	**imperméable** (m)	[ɛ̃pɛrmeabl]
waterproof (adj)	**imperméable** (adj)	[ɛ̃pɛrmeabl]

27. Men's & women's clothing

shirt	**chemise** (f)	[ʃəmiz]
pants	**pantalon** (m)	[pɑ̃talɔ̃]
jeans	**jean** (m)	[dʒin]
jacket (of man's suit)	**veston** (m)	[vɛstɔ̃]
suit	**complet** (m)	[kɔ̃plɛ]
dress (frock)	**robe** (f)	[rɔb]
skirt	**jupe** (f)	[ʒyp]
blouse	**chemisette** (f)	[ʃəmizɛt]
knitted jacket	**gilet** (m) **en laine**	[ʒilɛ ɑ̃ lɛn]
jacket (of woman's suit)	**jaquette** (f)	[ʒakɛt]
T-shirt	**tee-shirt** (m)	[tiʃœrt]
shorts (short trousers)	**short** (m)	[ʃɔrt]
tracksuit	**costume** (m) **de sport**	[kɔstym də spɔr]
bathrobe	**peignoir** (m) **de bain**	[pɛɲwar də bɛ̃]
pajamas	**pyjama** (m)	[piʒama]
sweater	**chandail** (m)	[ʃɑ̃daj]
pullover	**pull-over** (m)	[pylɔvɛr]
vest	**gilet** (m)	[ʒilɛ]
tailcoat	**queue-de-pie** (f)	[kødpi]
tuxedo	**smoking** (m)	[smɔkiŋ]
uniform	**uniforme** (m)	[ynifɔrm]

workwear	tenue (f) de travail	[təny də travaj]
overalls	salopette (f)	[salɔpɛt]
coat (e.g., doctor's smock)	blouse (f)	[bluz]

28. Clothing. Underwear

underwear	sous-vêtements (m pl)	[suvɛtmã]
boxers	boxer (m)	[bɔksɛr]
panties	slip (m) de femme	[slip də fam]
undershirt (A-shirt)	maillot (m) de corps	[majo də kɔr]
socks	chaussettes (f pl)	[ʃosɛt]

nightgown	chemise (f) de nuit	[ʃəmiz də nɥi]
bra	soutien-gorge (m)	[sutjɛ̃gɔrʒ]
knee highs	chaussettes (f pl) hautes	[ʃosɛt ot]
tights	collants (m pl)	[kɔlã]
stockings (thigh highs)	bas (m pl)	[ba]
bathing suit	maillot (m) de bain	[majo də bɛ̃]

29. Headwear

hat	bonnet (m)	[bɔnɛ]
fedora	chapeau (m) feutre	[ʃapo føtr]
baseball cap	casquette (f) de base-ball	[kaskɛt də bɛzbol]
flatcap	casquette (f)	[kaskɛt]

beret	béret (m)	[berɛ]
hood	capuche (f)	[kapyʃ]
panama hat	panama (m)	[panama]
knitted hat	bonnet (m) de laine	[bɔnɛ də lɛn]

| headscarf | foulard (m) | [fular] |
| women's hat | chapeau (m) de femme | [ʃapo də fam] |

hard hat	casque (m)	[kask]
garrison cap	calot (m)	[kalo]
helmet	casque (m)	[kask]

| derby | melon (m) | [məlõ] |
| top hat | haut-de-forme (m) | [o də fɔrm] |

30. Footwear

footwear	chaussures (f pl)	[ʃosyr]
ankle boots	bottines (f pl)	[botin]
shoes (low-heeled ~)	souliers (m pl)	[sulje]

boots (cowboy ~)	**bottes** (f pl)	[bɔt]
slippers	**chaussons** (m pl)	[ʃosɔ̃]
tennis shoes	**tennis** (m pl)	[tenis]
sneakers	**baskets** (f pl)	[baskɛt]
sandals	**sandales** (f pl)	[sɑ̃dal]
cobbler	**cordonnier** (m)	[kɔrdɔnje]
heel	**talon** (m)	[talɔ̃]
pair (of shoes)	**paire** (f)	[pɛr]
shoestring	**lacet** (m)	[lase]
to lace (vt)	**lacer** (vt)	[lase]
shoehorn	**chausse-pied** (m)	[ʃospje]
shoe polish	**cirage** (m)	[siraʒ]

31. Personal accessories

gloves	**gants** (m pl)	[gɑ̃]
mittens	**moufles** (f pl)	[mufl]
scarf (muffler)	**écharpe** (f)	[eʃarp]
glasses	**lunettes** (f pl)	[lynɛt]
frame (eyeglass ~)	**monture** (f)	[mɔ̃tyr]
umbrella	**parapluie** (m)	[paraplɥi]
walking stick	**canne** (f)	[kan]
hairbrush	**brosse** (f) **à cheveux**	[brɔs a ʃəvø]
fan	**éventail** (m)	[evɑ̃taj]
necktie	**cravate** (f)	[kravat]
bow tie	**nœud papillon** (m)	[nø papijɔ̃]
suspenders	**bretelles** (f pl)	[brətɛl]
handkerchief	**mouchoir** (m)	[muʃwar]
comb	**peigne** (m)	[pɛɲ]
barrette	**barrette** (f)	[barɛt]
hairpin	**épingle** (f) **à cheveux**	[epɛ̃gl a ʃəvø]
buckle	**boucle** (f)	[bukl]
belt	**ceinture** (f)	[sɛ̃tyr]
shoulder strap	**bandoulière** (f)	[bɑ̃duljɛr]
bag (handbag)	**sac** (m)	[sak]
purse	**sac** (m) **à main**	[sak a mɛ̃]
backpack	**sac** (m) **à dos**	[sak a do]

32. Clothing. Miscellaneous

fashion	**mode** (f)	[mɔd]
in vogue (adj)	**à la mode** (adj)	[alamɔd]

fashion designer	**couturier** (m)	[kutyrje]
collar	**col** (m)	[kɔl]
pocket	**poche** (f)	[pɔʃ]
pocket (as adj)	**de poche** (adj)	[də pɔʃ]
sleeve	**manche** (f)	[mɑ̃ʃ]
hanging loop	**bride** (f)	[brid]
fly (on trousers)	**braguette** (f)	[bragɛt]
zipper (fastener)	**fermeture** (f) **à glissière**	[fɛrmətyr a glisjɛr]
fastener	**agrafe** (f)	[agraf]
button	**bouton** (m)	[butɔ̃]
buttonhole	**boutonnière** (f)	[butɔnjɛr]
to come off (ab. button)	**s'arracher** (vp)	[saraʃe]
to sew (vi, vt)	**coudre** (vi, vt)	[kudr]
to embroider (vi, vt)	**broder** (vt)	[brɔde]
embroidery	**broderie** (f)	[brɔdri]
sewing needle	**aiguille** (f)	[egɥij]
thread	**fil** (m)	[fil]
seam	**couture** (f)	[kutyr]
to get dirty (vi)	**se salir** (vp)	[sə salir]
stain (mark, spot)	**tache** (f)	[taʃ]
to crease, crumple (vi)	**se froisser** (vp)	[sə frwase]
to tear (vt)	**déchirer** (vt)	[deʃire]
clothes moth	**mite** (f)	[mit]

33. Personal care. Cosmetics

toothpaste	**dentifrice** (m)	[dɑ̃tifris]
toothbrush	**brosse** (f) **à dents**	[brɔs a dɑ̃]
to brush one's teeth	**se brosser les dents**	[sə brɔse le dɑ̃]
razor	**rasoir** (m)	[razwar]
shaving cream	**crème** (f) **à raser**	[krɛm a raze]
to shave (vi)	**se raser** (vp)	[sə raze]
soap	**savon** (m)	[savɔ̃]
shampoo	**shampooing** (m)	[ʃɑ̃pwɛ̃]
scissors	**ciseaux** (m pl)	[sizo]
nail file	**lime** (f) **à ongles**	[lim a ɔ̃gl]
nail clippers	**pinces** (f pl) **à ongles**	[pɛ̃s a ɔ̃gl]
tweezers	**pince** (f)	[pɛ̃s]
cosmetics	**produits** (m pl) **de beauté**	[prɔdyi də bote]
face mask	**masque** (m) **de beauté**	[mask də bote]
manicure	**manucure** (f)	[manykyr]
to have a manicure	**se faire les ongles**	[sə fɛr le zɔ̃gl]
pedicure	**pédicurie** (f)	[pedikyri]

make-up bag	trousse (f) de toilette	[trus də twalɛt]
face powder	poudre (f)	[pudr]
powder compact	poudrier (m)	[pudrije]
blusher	fard (m) à joues	[far ɑ ʒu]

perfume (bottled)	parfum (m)	[parfœ̃]
toilet water (perfume)	eau (f) de toilette	[o də twalɛt]
lotion	lotion (f)	[losjɔ̃]
cologne	eau de Cologne (f)	[o də kɔlɔɲ]

eyeshadow	fard (m) à paupières	[far ɑ popjɛr]
eyeliner	crayon (m) à paupières	[krɛjɔ̃ ɑ popjɛr]
mascara	mascara (m)	[maskara]

lipstick	rouge (m) à lèvres	[ruʒ ɑ lɛvr]
nail polish, enamel	vernis (m) à ongles	[vɛrni ɑ ɔ̃gl]
hair spray	laque (f) pour les cheveux	[lak pur le ʃəvø]
deodorant	déodorant (m)	[deɔdɔrɑ̃]

cream	crème (f)	[krɛm]
face cream	crème (f) pour le visage	[krɛm pur lə vizaʒ]
hand cream	crème (f) pour les mains	[krɛm pur le mɛ̃]
anti-wrinkle cream	crème (f) anti-rides	[krɛm ɑ̃tirid]
day cream	crème (f) de jour	[krɛm də ʒur]
night cream	crème (f) de nuit	[krɛm də nɥi]
day (as adj)	de jour (adj)	[də ʒur]
night (as adj)	de nuit (adj)	[də nɥi]

tampon	tampon (m)	[tɑ̃pɔ̃]
toilet paper	papier (m) de toilette	[papje də twalɛt]
hair dryer	sèche-cheveux (m)	[sɛʃʃəvø]

34. Watches. Clocks

watch (wristwatch)	montre (f)	[mɔ̃tr]
dial	cadran (m)	[kadrɑ̃]
hand (of clock, watch)	aiguille (f)	[egɥij]
metal watch band	bracelet (m)	[braslɛ]
watch strap	bracelet (m)	[braslɛ]

battery	pile (f)	[pil]
to be dead (battery)	être déchargé	[ɛtr deʃarʒe]
to change a battery	changer de pile	[ʃɑ̃ʒe də pil]
to run fast	avancer (vi)	[avɑ̃se]
to run slow	retarder (vi)	[rətarde]

wall clock	pendule (f)	[pɑ̃dyl]
hourglass	sablier (m)	[sablije]
sundial	cadran (m) solaire	[kadrɑ̃ sɔlɛr]

alarm clock	**réveil** (m)	[revɛj]
watchmaker	**horloger** (m)	[ɔrlɔʒe]
to repair (vt)	**réparer** (vt)	[repare]

Food. Nutricion

35. Food

meat	viande (f)	[vjɑ̃d]
chicken	poulet (m)	[pulɛ]
young chicken	poulet (m)	[pulɛ]
duck	canard (m)	[kanar]
goose	oie (f)	[wa]
game	gibier (m)	[ʒibje]
turkey	dinde (f)	[dɛ̃d]

pork	du porc	[dy pɔr]
veal	du veau	[dy vo]
lamb	du mouton	[dy mutɔ̃]
beef	du bœuf	[dy bœf]
rabbit	lapin (m)	[lapɛ̃]

sausage (salami, etc.)	saucisson (m)	[sosisɔ̃]
vienna sausage	saucisse (f)	[sosis]
bacon	bacon (m)	[bekɔn]
ham	jambon (m)	[ʒɑ̃bɔ̃]
gammon (ham)	cuisse (f)	[kɥis]

pâté	pâté (m)	[pate]
liver	foie (m)	[fwa]
lard	lard (m)	[lar]
ground beef	farce (f)	[fars]
tongue	langue (f)	[lɑ̃g]

egg	œuf (m)	[œf]
eggs	les œufs	[lezø]
egg white	blanc (m) d'œuf	[blɑ̃ dœf]
egg yolk	jaune (m) d'œuf	[ʒon dœf]

fish	poisson (m)	[pwasɔ̃]
seafood	fruits (m pl) de mer	[frɥi də mɛr]
crustaceans	crustacés (m pl)	[krystase]
caviar	caviar (m)	[kavjar]

crab	crabe (m)	[krab]
shrimp	crevette (f)	[krəvɛt]

oyster	huître (f)	[ɥitr]
spiny lobster	langoustine (f)	[lɑ̃gustin]
octopus	poulpe (m)	[pulp]

squid	calamar (m)	[kalamar]
sturgeon	esturgeon (m)	[ɛstyrʒɔ̃]
salmon	saumon (m)	[somɔ̃]
halibut	flétan (m)	[fletɑ̃]

cod	morue (f)	[mɔry]
mackerel	maquereau (m)	[makro]
tuna	thon (m)	[tɔ̃]
eel	anguille (f)	[ɑ̃gij]

| trout | truite (f) | [trɥit] |
| sardine | sardine (f) | [sardin] |

| pike | brochet (m) | [brɔʃɛ] |
| herring | hareng (m) | [arɑ̃] |

| bread | pain (m) | [pɛ̃] |
| cheese | fromage (m) | [frɔmaʒ] |

| sugar | sucre (m) | [sykr] |
| salt | sel (m) | [sɛl] |

rice	riz (m)	[ri]
pasta	pâtes (m pl)	[pɑt]
noodles	nouilles (f pl)	[nuj]

butter	beurre (m)	[bœr]
vegetable oil	huile (f) végétale	[ɥil veʒetal]
sunflower oil	huile (f) de tournesol	[ɥil də turnəsɔl]
margarine	margarine (f)	[margarin]

| olives | olives (f pl) | [ɔliv] |
| olive oil | huile (f) d'olive | [ɥil dɔliv] |

milk	lait (m)	[lɛ]
condensed milk	lait (m) condensé	[lɛ kɔ̃dɑ̃se]
yogurt	yogourt (m)	[jaurt]

| sour cream | crème (f) aigre | [krɛm ɛgr] |
| cream (of milk) | crème (f) | [krɛm] |

| mayonnaise | sauce (f) mayonnaise | [sos majɔnɛz] |
| buttercream | crème (f) au beurre | [krɛm o bœr] |

cereal grain (wheat, etc.)	gruau (m)	[gryo]
flour	farine (f)	[farin]
canned food	conserves (f pl)	[kɔ̃sɛrv]

cornflakes	pétales (m pl) de maïs	[petal də mais]
honey	miel (m)	[mjɛl]
jam	confiture (f)	[kɔ̃fityr]
chewing gum	gomme (f) à mâcher	[gɔm a maʃe]

36. Drinks

water	eau (f)	[o]
drinking water	eau (f) potable	[o pɔtabl]
mineral water	eau (f) minérale	[o mineral]

still (adj)	plate (adj)	[plat]
carbonated (adj)	gazeuse (adj)	[gazøz]
sparkling (adj)	pétillante (adj)	[petijɑ̃t]
ice	glace (f)	[glas]
with ice	avec de la glace	[avɛk dəla glas]

non-alcoholic (adj)	sans alcool	[sɑ̃ zalkɔl]
soft drink	boisson (f) non alcoolisée	[bwasɔ̃ nonalkɔlize]
cool soft drink	rafraîchissement (m)	[rafrɛʃismɑ̃]
lemonade	limonade (f)	[limɔnad]

liquor	boissons (f pl) alcoolisées	[bwasɔ̃ alkɔlize]
wine	vin (m)	[vɛ̃]
white wine	vin (m) blanc	[vɛ̃ blɑ̃]
red wine	vin (m) rouge	[vɛ̃ ruʒ]

liqueur	liqueur (f)	[likœr]
champagne	champagne (m)	[ʃɑ̃paɲ]
vermouth	vermouth (m)	[vɛrmut]

whisky	whisky (m)	[wiski]
vodka	vodka (f)	[vɔdka]
gin	gin (m)	[dʒin]
cognac	cognac (m)	[kɔɲak]
rum	rhum (m)	[rɔm]

coffee	café (m)	[kafe]
black coffee	café (m) noir	[kafe nwar]
coffee with milk	café (m) au lait	[kafe o lɛ]
cappuccino	cappuccino (m)	[kaputʃino]
instant coffee	café (m) soluble	[kafe sɔlybl]

milk	lait (m)	[lɛ]
cocktail	cocktail (m)	[kɔktɛl]
milk shake	cocktail (m) au lait	[kɔktɛl o lɛ]

juice	jus (m)	[ʒy]
tomato juice	jus (m) de tomate	[ʒy də tɔmat]
orange juice	jus (m) d'orange	[ʒy dɔrɑ̃ʒ]
freshly squeezed juice	jus (m) pressé	[ʒy prese]

| beer | bière (f) | [bjɛr] |
| light beer | bière (f) blonde | [bjɛr blɔ̃d] |

dark beer	bière (f) brune	[bjɛr bryn]
tea	thé (m)	[te]
black tea	thé (m) noir	[te nwar]
green tea	thé (m) vert	[te vɛr]

37. Vegetables

| vegetables | légumes (m pl) | [legym] |
| greens | verdure (f) | [vɛrdyr] |

tomato	tomate (f)	[tɔmat]
cucumber	concombre (m)	[kɔ̃kɔ̃br]
carrot	carotte (f)	[karɔt]
potato	pomme (f) de terre	[pɔm də tɛr]
onion	oignon (m)	[ɔɲɔ̃]
garlic	ail (m)	[aj]

cabbage	chou (m)	[ʃu]
cauliflower	chou-fleur (m)	[ʃuflœr]
Brussels sprouts	chou (m) de Bruxelles	[ʃu də brysɛl]
broccoli	brocoli (m)	[brɔkɔli]

beetroot	betterave (f)	[bɛtrav]
eggplant	aubergine (f)	[obɛrʒin]
zucchini	courgette (f)	[kurʒɛt]
pumpkin	potiron (m)	[pɔtirɔ̃]
turnip	navet (m)	[navɛ]

parsley	persil (m)	[pɛrsi]
dill	fenouil (m)	[fənuj]
lettuce	laitue (f), salade (f)	[lety], [salad]
celery	céleri (m)	[sɛlri]
asparagus	asperge (f)	[aspɛrʒ]
spinach	épinard (m)	[epinar]

pea	pois (m)	[pwa]
beans	fèves (f pl)	[fɛv]
corn (maize)	maïs (m)	[mais]
kidney bean	haricot (m)	[ariko]

pepper	poivron (m)	[pwavrɔ̃]
radish	radis (m)	[radi]
artichoke	artichaut (m)	[artiʃo]

38. Fruits. Nuts

| fruit | fruit (m) | [frɥi] |
| apple | pomme (f) | [pɔm] |

pear	poire (f)	[pwar]
lemon	citron (m)	[sitrɔ̃]
orange	orange (f)	[ɔrɑ̃ʒ]
strawberry	fraise (f)	[frɛz]

mandarin	mandarine (f)	[mɑ̃darin]
plum	prune (f)	[pryn]
peach	pêche (f)	[pɛʃ]
apricot	abricot (m)	[abriko]
raspberry	framboise (f)	[frɑ̃bwaz]
pineapple	ananas (m)	[anana]

banana	banane (f)	[banan]
watermelon	pastèque (f)	[pastɛk]
grape	raisin (m)	[rɛzɛ̃]
sour cherry	cerise (f)	[səriz]
sweet cherry	merise (f)	[məriz]
melon	melon (m)	[məlɔ̃]

grapefruit	pamplemousse (m)	[pɑ̃pləmus]
avocado	avocat (m)	[avɔka]
papaya	papaye (f)	[papaj]
mango	mangue (f)	[mɑ̃g]
pomegranate	grenade (f)	[grənad]

redcurrant	groseille (f) rouge	[grozɛj ruʒ]
blackcurrant	cassis (m)	[kasis]
gooseberry	groseille (f) verte	[grozɛj vɛrt]
bilberry	myrtille (f)	[mirtij]
blackberry	mûre (f)	[myr]

raisin	raisin (m) sec	[rɛzɛ̃ sɛk]
fig	figue (f)	[fig]
date	datte (f)	[dat]

peanut	cacahuète (f)	[kakawɛt]
almond	amande (f)	[amɑ̃d]
walnut	noix (f)	[nwa]
hazelnut	noisette (f)	[nwazɛt]
coconut	noix (f) de coco	[nwa də kɔkɔ]
pistachios	pistaches (f pl)	[pistaʃ]

39. Bread. Candy

confectionery (pastry)	confiserie (f)	[kɔ̃fizri]
bread	pain (m)	[pɛ̃]
cookies	biscuit (m)	[biskɥi]

| chocolate (n) | chocolat (m) | [ʃɔkɔla] |
| chocolate (as adj) | en chocolat (adj) | [ɑ̃ ʃɔkɔla] |

candy	**bonbon** (m)	[bɔ̃bɔ̃]
cake (e.g., cupcake)	**gâteau** (m)	[gato]
cake (e.g., birthday ~)	**tarte** (f)	[tart]
pie (e.g., apple ~)	**gâteau** (m)	[gato]
filling (for cake, pie)	**garniture** (f)	[garnityr]
whole fruit jam	**confiture** (f)	[kɔ̃fityr]
marmalade	**marmelade** (f)	[marmǝlad]
waffle	**gaufre** (f)	[gofr]
ice-cream	**glace** (f)	[glas]
pudding	**pudding** (m)	[pudiŋ]

40. Cooked dishes

course, dish	**plat** (m)	[pla]
cuisine	**cuisine** (f)	[kɥizin]
recipe	**recette** (f)	[rǝsɛt]
portion	**portion** (f)	[pɔrsjɔ̃]
salad	**salade** (f)	[salad]
soup	**soupe** (f)	[sup]
clear soup (broth)	**bouillon** (m)	[bujɔ̃]
sandwich (bread)	**sandwich** (m)	[sãdwitʃ]
fried eggs	**les œufs brouillés**	[lezø bruje]
cutlet (croquette)	**boulette** (f)	[bulɛt]
hamburger (beefburger)	**hamburger** (m)	[ãbœrgœr]
beefsteak	**steak** (m)	[stɛk]
stew	**rôti** (m)	[roti]
side dish	**garniture** (f)	[garnityr]
spaghetti	**spaghettis** (m pl)	[spagɛti]
mashed potatoes	**purée** (f)	[pyre]
pizza	**pizza** (f)	[pidza]
porridge (oatmeal, etc.)	**bouillie** (f)	[buji]
omelet	**omelette** (f)	[ɔmlɛt]
boiled (e.g., ~ beef)	**cuit à l'eau** (adj)	[kɥitalo]
smoked (adj)	**fumé** (adj)	[fyme]
fried (adj)	**frit** (adj)	[fri]
dried (adj)	**sec** (adj)	[sɛk]
frozen (adj)	**congelé** (adj)	[kɔ̃ʒle]
pickled (adj)	**mariné** (adj)	[marine]
sweet (sugary)	**sucré** (adj)	[sykre]
salty (adj)	**salé** (adj)	[sale]
cold (adj)	**froid** (adj)	[frwa]
hot (adj)	**chaud** (adj)	[ʃo]

bitter (adj)	amer (adj)	[amɛr]
tasty (adj)	bon (adj)	[bɔ̃]

to cook in boiling water	cuire à l'eau	[kɥir a lo]
to cook (dinner)	préparer (vt)	[prepare]
to fry (vt)	faire frire	[fɛr frir]
to heat up (food)	réchauffer (vt)	[reʃofe]

to salt (vt)	saler (vt)	[sale]
to pepper (vt)	poivrer (vt)	[pwavre]
to grate (vt)	râper (vt)	[rɑpe]
peel (n)	peau (f)	[po]
to peel (vt)	éplucher (vt)	[eplyʃe]

41. Spices

salt	sel (m)	[sɛl]
salty (adj)	salé (adj)	[sale]
to salt (vt)	saler (vt)	[sale]

black pepper	poivre (m) noir	[pwavr nwar]
red pepper	poivre (m) rouge	[pwavr ruʒ]
mustard	moutarde (f)	[mutard]
horseradish	raifort (m)	[rɛfɔr]

condiment	condiment (m)	[kɔ̃dimɑ̃]
spice	épice (f)	[epis]
sauce	sauce (f)	[sos]
vinegar	vinaigre (m)	[vinɛgr]

anise	anis (m)	[ani(s)]
basil	basilic (m)	[bazilik]
cloves	clou (m) de girofle	[klu də ʒirɔfl]
ginger	gingembre (m)	[ʒɛ̃ʒɑ̃br]
coriander	coriandre (m)	[kɔrjɑ̃dr]
cinnamon	cannelle (f)	[kanɛl]

sesame	sésame (m)	[sezam]
bay leaf	feuille (f) de laurier	[fœj də lɔrje]
paprika	paprika (m)	[paprika]
caraway	cumin (m)	[kymɛ̃]
saffron	safran (m)	[safrɑ̃]

42. Meals

food	nourriture (f)	[nurityr]
to eat (vi, vt)	manger (vi, vt)	[mɑ̃ʒe]
breakfast	petit déjeuner (m)	[pəti deʒœne]

to have breakfast	prendre le petit déjeuner	[prɑ̃dr ləpti deʒœne]
lunch	déjeuner (m)	[deʒœne]
to have lunch	déjeuner (vi)	[deʒœne]
dinner	dîner (m)	[dine]
to have dinner	dîner (vi)	[dine]

| appetite | appétit (m) | [apeti] |
| Enjoy your meal! | Bon appétit! | [bɔn apeti] |

to open (~ a bottle)	ouvrir (vt)	[uvrir]
to spill (liquid)	renverser (vt)	[rɑ̃vɛrse]
to spill out (vi)	se renverser (vp)	[sə rɑ̃vɛrse]

to boil (vi)	bouillir (vi)	[bujir]
to boil (vt)	faire bouillir	[fɛr bujir]
boiled (~ water)	bouilli (adj)	[buji]
to chill, cool down (vt)	refroidir (vt)	[rəfrwadir]
to chill (vi)	se refroidir (vp)	[sə rəfrwadir]

| taste, flavor | goût (m) | [gu] |
| aftertaste | arrière-goût (m) | [arjɛrgu] |

to be on a diet	suivre un régime	[sɥivr œ̃ reʒim]
diet	régime (m)	[reʒim]
vitamin	vitamine (f)	[vitamin]
calorie	calorie (f)	[kalɔri]

| vegetarian (n) | végétarien (m) | [veʒetarjɛ̃] |
| vegetarian (adj) | végétarien (adj) | [veʒetarjɛ̃] |

fats (nutrient)	lipides (m pl)	[lipid]
proteins	protéines (f pl)	[prɔtein]
carbohydrates	glucides (m pl)	[glysid]

slice (of lemon, ham)	tranche (f)	[trɑ̃ʃ]
piece (of cake, pie)	morceau (m)	[mɔrso]
crumb (of bread)	miette (f)	[mjɛt]

43. Table setting

spoon	cuillère (f)	[kɥijɛr]
knife	couteau (m)	[kuto]
fork	fourchette (f)	[furʃɛt]

| cup (of coffee) | tasse (f) | [tɑs] |
| plate (dinner ~) | assiette (f) | [asjɛt] |

saucer	soucoupe (f)	[sukup]
napkin (on table)	serviette (f)	[sɛrvjɛt]
toothpick	cure-dent (m)	[kyrdɑ̃]

44. Restaurant

restaurant	restaurant (m)	[rɛstɔrɑ̃]
coffee house	salon (m) de café	[salɔ̃ də kafe]
pub, bar	bar (m)	[bar]
tearoom	salon (m) de thé	[salɔ̃ də te]
waiter	serveur (m)	[sɛrvœr]
waitress	serveuse (f)	[sɛrvøz]
bartender	barman (m)	[barman]
menu	carte (f)	[kart]
wine list	carte (f) des vins	[kart de vɛ̃]
to book a table	réserver une table	[rezɛrve yn tabl]
course, dish	plat (m)	[pla]
to order (meal)	commander (vt)	[kɔmɑ̃de]
to make an order	faire la commande	[fɛr la kɔmɑ̃d]
aperitif	apéritif (m)	[aperitif]
appetizer	hors-d'œuvre (m)	[ɔrdœvr]
dessert	dessert (m)	[desɛr]
check	addition (f)	[adisjɔ̃]
to pay the check	régler l'addition	[regle ladisjɔ̃]
to give change	rendre la monnaie	[rɑ̃dr la mɔnɛ]
tip	pourboire (m)	[purbwar]

Family, relatives and friends

45. Personal information. Forms

name, first name	**prénom** (m)	[prenɔ̃]
family name	**nom** (m) **de famille**	[nɔ̃ də famij]
date of birth	**date** (f) **de naissance**	[dat də nɛsɑ̃s]
place of birth	**lieu** (m) **de naissance**	[ljø də nɛsɑ̃s]
nationality	**nationalité** (f)	[nasjɔnalite]
place of residence	**domicile** (m)	[dɔmisil]
country	**pays** (m)	[pei]
profession (occupation)	**profession** (f)	[prɔfɛsjɔ̃]
gender, sex	**sexe** (m)	[sɛks]
height	**taille** (f)	[taj]
weight	**poids** (m)	[pwa]

46. Family members. Relatives

mother	**mère** (f)	[mɛr]
father	**père** (m)	[pɛr]
son	**fils** (m)	[fis]
daughter	**fille** (f)	[fij]
younger daughter	**fille** (f) **cadette**	[fij kadɛt]
younger son	**fils** (m) **cadet**	[fis kadɛ]
eldest daughter	**fille** (f) **aînée**	[fij ene]
eldest son	**fils** (m) **aîné**	[fis ene]
brother	**frère** (m)	[frɛr]
sister	**sœur** (f)	[sœr]
cousin (masc.)	**cousin** (m)	[kuzɛ̃]
cousin (fem.)	**cousine** (f)	[kuzin]
mom	**maman** (f)	[mamɑ̃]
dad, daddy	**papa** (m)	[papa]
parents	**parents** (pl)	[parɑ̃]
child	**enfant** (m, f)	[ɑ̃fɑ̃]
children	**enfants** (pl)	[ɑ̃fɑ̃]
grandmother	**grand-mère** (f)	[grɑ̃mɛr]
grandfather	**grand-père** (m)	[grɑ̃pɛr]
grandson	**petit-fils** (m)	[pti fis]

granddaughter	**petite-fille** (f)	[ptit fij]
grandchildren	**petits-enfants** (pl)	[pətizɑ̃fɑ̃]
uncle	**oncle** (m)	[ɔ̃kl]
aunt	**tante** (f)	[tɑ̃t]
nephew	**neveu** (m)	[nəvø]
niece	**nièce** (f)	[njɛs]
mother-in-law (wife's mother)	**belle-mère** (f)	[bɛlmɛr]
father-in-law (husband's father)	**beau-père** (m)	[bopɛr]
son-in-law (daughter's husband)	**gendre** (m)	[ʒɑ̃dr]
stepmother	**belle-mère, marâtre** (f)	[bɛlmɛr], [marɑtr]
stepfather	**beau-père** (m)	[bopɛr]
infant	**nourrisson** (m)	[nurisɔ̃]
baby (infant)	**bébé** (m)	[bebe]
little boy, kid	**petit** (m)	[pti]
wife	**femme** (f)	[fam]
husband	**mari** (m)	[mari]
spouse (husband)	**époux** (m)	[epu]
spouse (wife)	**épouse** (f)	[epuz]
married (masc.)	**marié** (adj)	[marje]
married (fem.)	**mariée** (adj)	[marje]
single (unmarried)	**célibataire** (adj)	[selibatɛr]
bachelor	**célibataire** (m)	[selibatɛr]
divorced (masc.)	**divorcé** (adj)	[divorse]
widow	**veuve** (f)	[vœv]
widower	**veuf** (m)	[vœf]
relative	**parent** (m)	[parɑ̃]
close relative	**parent** (m) **proche**	[parɑ̃ prɔʃ]
distant relative	**parent** (m) **éloigné**	[parɑ̃ elwaɲe]
relatives	**parents** (m pl)	[parɑ̃]
orphan (boy)	**orphelin** (m)	[ɔrfəlɛ̃]
orphan (girl)	**orpheline** (f)	[ɔrfəlin]
guardian (of minor)	**tuteur** (m)	[tytœr]
to adopt (a boy)	**adopter** (vt)	[adɔpte]
to adopt (a girl)	**adopter** (vt)	[adɔpte]

Medicine

47. Diseases

sickness	maladie (f)	[maladi]
to be sick	être malade	[ɛtr malad]
health	santé (f)	[sɑ̃te]
runny nose (coryza)	rhume (m)	[rym]
angina	angine (f)	[ɑ̃ʒin]
cold (illness)	refroidissement (m)	[rəfrwadismɑ̃]
to catch a cold	prendre froid	[prɑ̃dr frwa]
bronchitis	bronchite (f)	[brɔ̃ʃit]
pneumonia	pneumonie (f)	[pnømɔni]
flu, influenza	grippe (f)	[grip]
near-sighted (adj)	myope (adj)	[mjɔp]
far-sighted (adj)	presbyte (adj)	[prɛsbit]
strabismus (crossed eyes)	strabisme (m)	[strabism]
cross-eyed (adj)	strabique (adj)	[strabik]
cataract	cataracte (f)	[katarakt]
glaucoma	glaucome (m)	[glokom]
stroke	insulte (f)	[ɛ̃sylt]
heart attack	crise (f) cardiaque	[kriz kardjak]
myocardial infarction	infarctus (m) de myocarde	[ɛ̃farktys də mjɔkard]
paralysis	paralysie (f)	[paralizi]
to paralyze (vt)	paralyser (vt)	[paralize]
allergy	allergie (f)	[alɛrʒi]
asthma	asthme (m)	[asm]
diabetes	diabète (m)	[djabɛt]
toothache	mal (m) de dents	[mal də dɑ̃]
caries	carie (f)	[kari]
diarrhea	diarrhée (f)	[djare]
constipation	constipation (f)	[kɔ̃stipasjɔ̃]
stomach upset	estomac (m) barbouillé	[ɛstɔma barbuje]
food poisoning	intoxication (f) alimentaire	[ɛ̃tɔksikasjɔn alimɑ̃tɛr]
to have a food poisoning	être intoxiqué	[ɛtr ɛ̃tɔksike]
arthritis	arthrite (f)	[artrit]
rickets	rachitisme (m)	[raʃitism]

rheumatism	rhumatisme (m)	[rymatism]
atherosclerosis	athérosclérose (f)	[ateroskleroz]

gastritis	gastrite (f)	[gastrit]
appendicitis	appendicite (f)	[apɛ̃disit]
cholecystitis	cholécystite (f)	[kɔlesistit]
ulcer	ulcère (m)	[ylsɛr]

measles	rougeole (f)	[ruʒɔl]
German measles	rubéole (f)	[rybeɔl]
jaundice	jaunisse (f)	[ʒonis]
hepatitis	hépatite (f)	[epatit]

schizophrenia	schizophrénie (f)	[skizɔfreni]
rabies (hydrophobia)	rage (f)	[raʒ]
neurosis	névrose (f)	[nevroz]
concussion	commotion (f) cérébrale	[kɔmɔsjɔ̃ serebral]

cancer	cancer (m)	[kɑ̃sɛr]
sclerosis	sclérose (f)	[skleroz]
multiple sclerosis	sclérose (f) en plaques	[skleroz ɑ̃ plak]

alcoholism	alcoolisme (m)	[alkɔlism]
alcoholic (n)	alcoolique (m)	[alkɔlik]
syphilis	syphilis (f)	[sifilis]
AIDS	SIDA (m)	[sida]

tumor	tumeur (f)	[tymœr]
malignant (adj)	maligne (adj)	[maliɲ]
benign (adj)	bénigne (adj)	[beniɲ]

fever	fièvre (f)	[fjɛvr]
malaria	malaria (f)	[malarja]
gangrene	gangrène (f)	[gɑ̃grɛn]
seasickness	mal (m) de mer	[mal də mɛr]
epilepsy	épilepsie (f)	[epilɛpsi]

epidemic	épidémie (f)	[epidemi]
typhus	typhus (m)	[tifys]
tuberculosis	tuberculose (f)	[tybɛrkyloz]
cholera	choléra (m)	[kɔlera]
plague (bubonic ~)	peste (f)	[pɛst]

48. Symptoms. Treatments. Part 1

symptom	symptôme (m)	[sɛ̃ptom]
temperature	température (f)	[tɑ̃peratyr]
high temperature	fièvre (f)	[fjɛvr]
pulse	pouls (m)	[pu]

giddiness	vertige (m)	[vɛrtiʒ]
hot (adj)	chaud (adj)	[ʃo]
shivering	frisson (m)	[frisõ]
pale (e.g., ~ face)	pâle (adj)	[pɑl]

cough	toux (f)	[tu]
to cough (vi)	tousser (vi)	[tuse]
to sneeze (vi)	éternuer (vi)	[etɛrnɥe]
faint	évanouissement (m)	[evanwismɑ̃]
to faint (vi)	s'évanouir (vp)	[sevanwir]

bruise (hématome)	bleu (m)	[blø]
bump (lump)	bosse (f)	[bɔs]
to bruise oneself	se heurter (vp)	[sə œrte]
bruise (contusion)	meurtrissure (f)	[mœrtrisyr]
to get bruised	se faire mal	[sə fɛr mal]

to limp (vi)	boiter (vi)	[bwate]
dislocation	foulure (f)	[fulyr]
to dislocate (vt)	se démettre (vp)	[sə demɛtr]
fracture	fracture (f)	[fraktyr]
to have a fracture	avoir une fracture	[avwar yn fraktyr]

cut (e.g., paper ~)	coupure (f)	[kupyr]
to cut oneself	se couper (vp)	[sə kupe]
bleeding	hémorragie (f)	[emɔraʒi]

| burn (injury) | brûlure (f) | [brylyr] |
| to scald oneself | se brûler (vp) | [sə bryle] |

to prick (vt)	se piquer (vp)	[sə pike]
to prick oneself	se piquer (vp)	[sə pike]
to injure (vt)	blesser (vt)	[blese]
injury	blessure (f)	[blesyr]
wound	blessure (f)	[blesyr]
trauma	trauma (m)	[troma]

to be delirious	délirer (vi)	[delire]
to stutter (vi)	bégayer (vi)	[begeje]
sunstroke	insolation (f)	[ɛ̃sɔlasjõ]

49. Symptoms. Treatments. Part 2

| pain | douleur (f) | [dulœr] |
| splinter (in foot, etc.) | écharde (f) | [eʃard] |

sweat (perspiration)	sueur (f)	[sɥœr]
to sweat (perspire)	suer (vi)	[sɥe]
vomiting	vomissement (m)	[vɔmismɑ̃]
convulsions	spasmes (m pl)	[spasm]

pregnant (adj)	enceinte (adj)	[ãsɛ̃t]
to be born	naître (vi)	[nɛtr]
delivery, labor	accouchement (m)	[akuʃmã]
to deliver (~ a baby)	accoucher (vt)	[akuʃe]
abortion	avortement (m)	[avɔrtəmã]
breathing, respiration	respiration (f)	[rɛspirasjɔ̃]
inhalation	inhalation (f)	[inalasjɔ̃]
exhalation	expiration (f)	[ɛkspirasjɔ̃]
to exhale (vi)	expirer (vi)	[ɛkspire]
to inhale (vi)	inspirer (vi)	[inale]
disabled person	invalide (m)	[ɛ̃valid]
cripple	handicapé (m)	[ãdikape]
drug addict	drogué (m)	[drɔge]
deaf (adj)	sourd (adj)	[sur]
dumb, mute	muet (adj)	[mɥɛ]
deaf-and-dumb (adj)	sourd-muet (adj)	[surmɥɛ]
mad, insane (adj)	fou (adj)	[fu]
madman	fou (m)	[fu]
madwoman	folle (f)	[fɔl]
to go insane	devenir fou	[dəvnir fu]
gene	gène (m)	[ʒɛn]
immunity	immunité (f)	[imynite]
hereditary (adj)	héréditaire (adj)	[ereditɛr]
congenital (adj)	congénital (adj)	[kɔ̃ʒenital]
virus	virus (m)	[virys]
microbe	microbe (m)	[mikrɔb]
bacterium	bactérie (f)	[bakteri]
infection	infection (f)	[ɛ̃fɛksjɔ̃]

50. Symptoms. Treatments. Part 3

hospital	hôpital (m)	[ɔpital]
patient	patient (m)	[pasjã]
diagnosis	diagnostic (m)	[djagnɔstik]
cure	cure (f)	[kyr]
medical treatment	traitement (m)	[trɛtmã]
to get treatment	se faire soigner	[sə fɛr swaɲe]
to treat (vt)	traiter (vt)	[trete]
to nurse (look after)	soigner (vt)	[swaɲe]
care (nursing ~)	soins (m pl)	[swɛ̃]
operation, surgery	opération (f)	[ɔperasjɔ̃]
to bandage (head, limb)	panser (vt)	[pãse]

bandaging	pansement (m)	[pɑ̃smɑ̃]
vaccination	vaccination (f)	[vaksinasjɔ̃]
to vaccinate (vt)	vacciner (vt)	[vaksine]
injection, shot	piqûre (f)	[pikyr]
to give an injection	faire une piqûre	[fɛr yn pikyr]

attack	crise, attaque (f)	[kriz], [atak]
amputation	amputation (f)	[ɑ̃pytasjɔ̃]
to amputate (vt)	amputer (vt)	[ɑ̃pyte]
coma	coma (m)	[kɔma]
to be in a coma	être dans le coma	[ɛtr dɑ̃ lə kɔma]
intensive care	réanimation (f)	[reanimasjɔ̃]

to recover (~ from flu)	se rétablir (vp)	[sə retablir]
state (patient's ~)	état (m)	[eta]
consciousness	conscience (f)	[kɔ̃sjɑ̃s]
memory (faculty)	mémoire (f)	[memwar]

to extract (tooth)	arracher (vt)	[araʃe]
filling	plombage (m)	[plɔ̃baʒ]
to fill (a tooth)	plomber (vt)	[plɔ̃be]

hypnosis	hypnose (f)	[ipnoz]
to hypnotize (vt)	hypnotiser (vt)	[ipnɔtize]

51. Doctors

doctor	médecin (m)	[medsɛ̃]
nurse	infirmière (f)	[ɛ̃firmjɛr]
private physician	médecin (m) personnel	[medsɛ̃ pɛrsɔnɛl]

dentist	dentiste (m)	[dɑ̃tist]
ophthalmologist	ophtalmologiste (m)	[ɔftalmɔlɔʒist]
internist	généraliste (m)	[ʒeneralist]
surgeon	chirurgien (m)	[ʃiryrʒjɛ̃]

psychiatrist	psychiatre (m)	[psikjatr]
pediatrician	pédiatre (m)	[pedjatr]
psychologist	psychologue (m)	[psikɔlɔg]
gynecologist	gynécologue (m)	[ʒinekɔlɔg]
cardiologist	cardiologue (m)	[kardjɔlɔg]

52. Medicine. Drugs. Accessories

medicine, drug	médicament (m)	[medikamɑ̃]
remedy	remède (m)	[rəmɛd]
to prescribe (vt)	prescrire (vt)	[prɛskrir]
prescription	ordonnance (f)	[ɔrdɔnɑ̃s]

tablet, pill	comprimé (m)	[kɔ̃prime]
ointment	onguent (m)	[ɔ̃gɑ̃]
ampule	ampoule (f)	[ɑ̃pul]
mixture	mixture (f)	[mikstyr]
syrup	sirop (m)	[siro]
pill	pilule (f)	[pilyl]
powder	poudre (f)	[pudr]
bandage	bande (f)	[bɑ̃d]
cotton wool	coton (m)	[kɔtɔ̃]
iodine	iode (m)	[jɔd]
Band-Aid	sparadrap (m)	[sparadra]
eyedropper	compte-gouttes (m)	[kɔ̃tgut]
thermometer	thermomètre (m)	[tɛrmɔmɛtr]
syringe	seringue (f)	[sərɛ̃g]
wheelchair	fauteuil (m) roulant	[fotœj rulɑ̃]
crutches	béquilles (f pl)	[bekij]
painkiller	anesthésique (m)	[anɛstezik]
laxative	purgatif (m)	[pyrgatif]
spirit (ethanol)	alcool (m)	[alkɔl]
medicinal herbs	herbe (f) médicinale	[ɛrb medisinal]
herbal (~ tea)	d'herbes (adj)	[dɛrb]

HUMAN HABITAT

City

53. City. Life in the city

city, town	**ville** (f)	[vil]
capital city	**capitale** (f)	[kapital]
village	**village** (m)	[vilaʒ]
city map	**plan** (m) **de la ville**	[plɑ̃ də la vil]
downtown	**centre-ville** (m)	[sɑ̃trəvil]
suburb	**banlieue** (f)	[bɑ̃ljø]
suburban (adj)	**de banlieue** (adj)	[də bɑ̃ljø]
outskirts	**périphérie** (f)	[periferi]
environs (suburbs)	**alentours** (m pl)	[alɑ̃tur]
city block	**quartier** (m)	[kartje]
residential block	**quartier** (m) **résidentiel**	[kartje rezidɑ̃sjɛl]
traffic	**trafic** (m)	[trafik]
traffic lights	**feux** (m pl) **de circulation**	[fø də sirkylasjɔ̃]
public transportation	**transport** (m) **urbain**	[trɑ̃spɔr yrbɛ̃]
intersection	**carrefour** (m)	[karfur]
crosswalk	**passage** (m) **piéton**	[pɑsaʒ pjetɔ̃]
pedestrian underpass	**passage** (m) **souterrain**	[pɑsaʒ sutɛrɛ̃]
to cross (vt)	**traverser** (vt)	[travɛrse]
pedestrian	**piéton** (m)	[pjetɔ̃]
sidewalk	**trottoir** (m)	[trɔtwar]
bridge	**pont** (m)	[pɔ̃]
bank (riverbank)	**quai** (m)	[kɛ]
fountain	**fontaine** (f)	[fɔ̃tɛn]
allée	**allée** (f)	[ale]
park	**parc** (m)	[park]
boulevard	**boulevard** (m)	[bulvar]
square	**place** (f)	[plas]
avenue (wide street)	**avenue** (f)	[avny]
street	**rue** (f)	[ry]
side street	**ruelle** (f)	[rɥɛl]
dead end	**impasse** (f)	[ɛ̃pas]
house	**maison** (f)	[mɛzɔ̃]
building	**édifice** (m)	[edifis]

skyscraper	gratte-ciel (m)	[gratsjɛl]
facade	façade (f)	[fasad]
roof	toit (m)	[twa]
window	fenêtre (f)	[fənɛtr]
arch	arc (m)	[ark]
column	colonne (f)	[kɔlɔn]
corner	coin (m)	[kwɛ̃]

store window	vitrine (f)	[vitrin]
store sign	enseigne (f)	[ɑ̃sɛɲ]
poster	affiche (f)	[afiʃ]
advertising poster	affiche (f) publicitaire	[afiʃ pyblisitɛr]
billboard	panneau-réclame (m)	[pano reklam]

garbage, trash	ordures (f pl)	[ɔrdyr]
garbage can	poubelle (f)	[pubɛl]
to litter (vi)	jeter ... à terre	[ʒəte ... ɑ tɛr]
garbage dump	décharge (f)	[deʃarʒ]

phone booth	cabine (f) téléphonique	[kabin telefɔnik]
lamppost	réverbère (m)	[revɛrbɛr]
bench (park ~)	banc (m)	[bɑ̃]

police officer	policier (m)	[pɔlisje]
police	police (f)	[pɔlis]
beggar	clochard (m)	[klɔʃar]
homeless, bum	sans-abri (m)	[sɑ̃zabri]

54. Urban institutions

store	magasin (m)	[magazɛ̃]
drugstore, pharmacy	pharmacie (f)	[farmasi]
optical store	opticien (m)	[ɔptisjɛ̃]
shopping mall	centre (m) commercial	[sɑ̃tr kɔmɛrsjal]
supermarket	supermarché (m)	[sypɛrmarʃe]

bakery	boulangerie (f)	[bulɑ̃ʒri]
baker	boulanger (m)	[bulɑ̃ʒe]
candy store	pâtisserie (f)	[pɑtisri]
grocery store	épicerie (f)	[episri]
butcher shop	boucherie (f)	[buʃri]

| produce store | magasin (m) de légumes | [magazɛ̃ də legym] |
| market | marché (m) | [marʃe] |

coffee house	salon (m) de café	[salɔ̃ də kafe]
restaurant	restaurant (m)	[rɛstɔrɑ̃]
pub	brasserie (f)	[brasri]
pizzeria	pizzeria (f)	[pidzerja]
hair salon	salon (m) de coiffure	[salɔ̃ də kwafyr]

post office	**poste** (f)	[pɔst]
dry cleaners	**pressing** (m)	[presiŋ]
photo studio	**atelier** (m) **de photo**	[atəlje də fɔto]

shoe store	**magasin** (m) **de chaussures**	[magazɛ̃ də ʃosyr]
bookstore	**librairie** (f)	[librɛri]
sporting goods store	**magasin** (m) **d'articles de sport**	[magazɛ̃ dartikl də spɔr]

clothes repair	**atelier** (m) **de retouche**	[atəlje də rətuʃ]
formal wear rental	**location** (f) **de vêtements**	[lɔkasjɔ̃ də vɛtmɑ̃]
movie rental store	**location** (f) **de films**	[lɔkasjɔ̃ də film]

circus	**cirque** (m)	[sirk]
zoo	**zoo** (m)	[zoo]
movie theater	**cinéma** (m)	[sinema]
museum	**musée** (m)	[myze]
library	**bibliothèque** (f)	[biblijɔtɛk]

theater	**théâtre** (m)	[teatr]
opera	**opéra** (m)	[ɔpera]
nightclub	**boîte** (f) **de nuit**	[bwat də nɥi]
casino	**casino** (m)	[kazino]

mosque	**mosquée** (f)	[mɔske]
synagogue	**synagogue** (f)	[sinagɔg]
cathedral	**cathédrale** (f)	[katedral]
temple	**temple** (m)	[tɑ̃pl]
church	**église** (f)	[egliz]

college	**institut** (m)	[ɛ̃stity]
university	**université** (f)	[ynivɛrsite]
school	**école** (f)	[ekɔl]

prefecture	**préfecture** (f)	[prefɛktyr]
city hall	**mairie** (f)	[meri]
hotel	**hôtel** (m)	[otɛl]
bank	**banque** (f)	[bɑ̃k]

| embassy | **ambassade** (f) | [ɑ̃basad] |
| travel agency | **agence** (f) **de voyages** | [aʒɑ̃s də vwajaʒ] |

| information office | **bureau** (m) **d'information** | [byro dɛ̃fɔrmasjɔ̃] |
| money exchange | **bureau** (m) **de change** | [byro də ʃɑ̃ʒ] |

| subway | **métro** (m) | [metro] |
| hospital | **hôpital** (m) | [ɔpital] |

| gas station | **station-service** (f) | [stasjɔ̃sɛrvis] |
| parking lot | **parking** (m) | [parkiŋ] |

55. Signs

store sign	enseigne (f)	[ãsɛɲ]
notice (written text)	pancarte (f)	[pãkart]
poster	poster (m)	[pɔstɛr]
direction sign	indicateur (m) de direction	[ɛ̃dikatœr də dirɛksjõ]
arrow (sign)	flèche (f)	[flɛʃ]
caution	avertissement (m)	[avɛrtismã]
warning sign	panneau (m) d'avertissement	[pano davɛrtismã]
to warn (vt)	avertir (vt)	[avɛrtir]
day off	jour (m) de repos	[ʒur də rəpo]
timetable (schedule)	horaire (m)	[ɔrɛr]
opening hours	heures (f pl) d'ouverture	[zœr duvɛrtyr]
WELCOME!	BIENVENUE!	[bjɛ̃vny]
ENTRANCE	ENTRÉE	[ãtre]
EXIT	SORTIE	[sɔrti]
PUSH	POUSSER	[puse]
PULL	TIRER	[tire]
OPEN	OUVERT	[uvɛr]
CLOSED	FERMÉ	[fɛrme]
WOMEN	FEMMES	[fam]
MEN	HOMMES	[ɔm]
DISCOUNTS	RABAIS	[sɔld]
SALE	SOLDES	[rabɛ]
NEW!	NOUVEAU!	[nuvo]
FREE	GRATUIT	[gratɥi]
ATTENTION!	ATTENTION!	[atãsjõ]
NO VACANCIES	COMPLET	[kõplɛ]
RESERVED	RÉSERVÉ	[rezɛrve]
ADMINISTRATION	ADMINISTRATION	[administrasjõ]
STAFF ONLY	RÉSERVÉ AU PERSONNEL	[rezɛrve o pɛrsɔnɛl]
BEWARE OF THE DOG!	ATTENTION CHIEN MÉCHANT	[atãsjõ ʃjɛ̃ meʃã]
NO SMOKING	DÉFENSE DE FUMER	[defãs də fyme]
DO NOT TOUCH!	PRIERE DE NE PAS TOUCHER	[prijɛr dənəpɑ tuʃe]
DANGEROUS	DANGEREUX	[dãʒrø]
DANGER	DANGER	[dãʒe]

HIGH TENSION	HAUTE TENSION	[ot tɑ̃sjɔ̃]
NO SWIMMING!	BAIGNADE INTERDITE	[bɛɲad ɛ̃tɛrdit]
OUT OF ORDER	HORS SERVICE	[ɔr sɛrvis]

FLAMMABLE	INFLAMMABLE	[ɛ̃flamabl]
FORBIDDEN	INTERDIT	[ɛ̃tɛrdi]
NO TRESPASSING!	PASSAGE INTERDIT	[pɑsaʒ ɛ̃tɛrdi]
WET PAINT	PEINTURE FRAÎCHE	[pɛ̃tyr frɛʃ]

56. Urban transportation

bus	autobus (m)	[otobys]
streetcar	tramway (m)	[tramwɛ]
trolley	trolleybus (m)	[trɔlɛbys]
route (of bus)	itinéraire (m)	[itinerɛr]
number (e.g., bus ~)	numéro (m)	[nymero]

to go by ...	prendre ...	[prɑ̃dr]
to get on (~ the bus)	monter (vi)	[mɔ̃te]
to get off ...	descendre de ...	[desɑ̃dr də]

stop (e.g., bus ~)	arrêt (m)	[arɛ]
next stop	arrêt (m) prochain	[arɛt prɔʃɛ̃]
terminus	terminus (m)	[tɛrminys]
schedule	horaire (m)	[ɔrɛr]
to wait (vt)	attendre (vt)	[atɑ̃dr]

| ticket | ticket (m) | [tikɛ] |
| fare | prix (m) du ticket | [pri dy tikɛ] |

cashier (ticket seller)	caissier (m)	[kesje]
ticket inspection	contrôle (m) des tickets	[kɔ̃trol de tikɛ]
conductor	contrôleur (m)	[kɔ̃trolœr]

to be late (for ...)	être en retard	[ɛtr ɑ̃ rətar]
to miss (~ the train, etc.)	rater (vt)	[rate]
to be in a hurry	se dépêcher	[sə depeʃe]

taxi, cab	taxi (m)	[taksi]
taxi driver	chauffeur (m) de taxi	[ʃofœr də taksi]
by taxi	en taxi	[ɑ̃ taksi]
taxi stand	arrêt (m) de taxi	[arɛ də taksi]
to call a taxi	appeler un taxi	[aple œ̃ taksi]
to take a taxi	prendre un taxi	[prɑ̃dr œ̃ taksi]

traffic	trafic (m)	[trafik]
traffic jam	embouteillage (m)	[ɑ̃butɛjaʒ]
rush hour	heures (f pl) de pointe	[œr də pwɛ̃t]
to park (vi)	se garer (vp)	[sə gare]

| to park (vt) | garer (vt) | [gare] |
| parking lot | parking (m) | [parkiŋ] |

subway	métro (m)	[metro]
station	station (f)	[stasjɔ̃]
to take the subway	prendre le métro	[prɑ̃dr lə metro]
train	train (m)	[trɛ̃]
train station	gare (f)	[gar]

57. Sightseeing

monument	monument (m)	[mɔnymɑ̃]
fortress	forteresse (f)	[fɔrtərɛs]
palace	palais (m)	[palɛ]
castle	château (m)	[ʃato]
tower	tour (f)	[tur]
mausoleum	mausolée (m)	[mozɔle]

architecture	architecture (f)	[arʃitɛktyr]
medieval (adj)	médiéval (adj)	[medjeval]
ancient (adj)	ancien (adj)	[ɑ̃sjɛ̃]
national (adj)	national (adj)	[nasjɔnal]
well-known (adj)	connu (adj)	[kɔny]

tourist	touriste (m)	[turist]
guide (person)	guide (m)	[gid]
excursion, guided tour	excursion (f)	[ɛkskyrsjɔ̃]
to show (vt)	montrer (vt)	[mɔ̃tre]
to tell (vt)	raconter (vt)	[rakɔ̃te]

to find (vt)	trouver (vt)	[truve]
to get lost (lose one's way)	se perdre (vp)	[sə pɛrdr]
map (e.g., subway ~)	plan (m)	[plɑ̃]
map (e.g., city ~)	carte (f)	[kart]

souvenir, gift	souvenir (m)	[suvnir]
gift shop	boutique (f) de souvenirs	[butik də suvnir]
to take pictures	prendre en photo	[prɑ̃dr ɑ̃ fɔto]
to be photographed	se faire prendre en photo	[sə fɛr prɑ̃dr ɑ̃ fɔto]

58. Shopping

to buy (purchase)	acheter (vt)	[aʃte]
purchase	achat (m)	[aʃa]
to go shopping	faire des achats	[fɛr dezaʃa]
shopping	shopping (m)	[ʃɔpiŋ]
to be open (ab. store)	être ouvert	[ɛtr uvɛr]

to be closed	être fermé	[ɛtr fɛrme]
footwear	chaussures (f pl)	[ʃosyr]
clothes, clothing	vêtement (m)	[vɛtmɑ̃]
cosmetics	produits (m pl) de beauté	[prɔdyi də bote]
food products	produits (m pl) alimentaires	[prɔdyi alimɑ̃tɛr]
gift, present	cadeau (m)	[kado]
salesman	vendeur (m)	[vɑ̃dœr]
saleswoman	vendeuse (f)	[vɑ̃døz]
check out, cash desk	caisse (f)	[kɛs]
mirror	miroir (m)	[mirwar]
counter (in shop)	comptoir (m)	[kɔ̃twar]
fitting room	cabine (f) d'essayage	[kabin desɛjaʒ]
to try on	essayer (vt)	[eseje]
to fit (ab. dress, etc.)	aller bien	[ale bjɛ̃]
to like (I like ...)	plaire à ...	[plɛr a]
price	prix (m)	[pri]
price tag	étiquette (f) de prix	[etikɛt də pri]
to cost (vt)	coûter (vi, vt)	[kute]
How much?	Combien?	[kɔ̃bjɛ̃]
discount	rabais (m)	[rabɛ]
inexpensive (adj)	pas cher (adj)	[pɑ ʃɛr]
cheap (adj)	bon marché (adj)	[bɔ̃ marʃe]
expensive (adj)	cher (adj)	[ʃɛr]
It's expensive	C'est cher	[sɛ ʃɛr]
rental (n)	location (f)	[lɔkasjɔ̃]
to rent (~ a tuxedo)	louer (vt)	[lwe]
credit	crédit (m)	[kredi]
on credit (adv)	à crédit (adv)	[akredi]

59. Money

money	argent (m)	[arʒɑ̃]
currency exchange	échange (m)	[eʃɑ̃ʒ]
exchange rate	cours (m) de change	[kur də ʃɑ̃ʒ]
ATM	distributeur (m)	[distribytœr]
coin	monnaie (f)	[mɔnɛ]
dollar	dollar (m)	[dɔlar]
euro	euro (m)	[øro]
lira	lire (f)	[lir]
Deutschmark	mark (m) allemand	[mark almɑ̃]
franc	franc (m)	[frɑ̃]

pound sterling	**livre sterling** (f)	[livr stɛrliŋ]
yen	**yen** (m)	[jɛn]
debt	**dette** (f)	[dɛt]
debtor	**débiteur** (m)	[debitœr]
to lend (money)	**prêter** (vt)	[prete]
to borrow (vi, vt)	**emprunter** (vt)	[ɑ̃prœ̃te]
bank	**banque** (f)	[bɑ̃k]
account	**compte** (m)	[kɔ̃t]
to deposit (vt)	**verser** (vt)	[vɛrse]
to deposit into the account	**verser dans le compte**	[vɛrse dɑ̃ lə kɔ̃t]
to withdraw (vt)	**retirer du compte**	[rətire dy kɔ̃t]
credit card	**carte** (f) **de crédit**	[kart də kredi]
cash	**espèces** (f pl)	[ɛspɛs]
check	**chèque** (m)	[ʃɛk]
to write a check	**faire un chèque**	[fɛr œ̃ ʃɛk]
checkbook	**chéquier** (m)	[ʃekje]
wallet	**portefeuille** (m)	[pɔrtəfœj]
change purse	**bourse** (f)	[burs]
billfold	**porte-monnaie** (m)	[pɔrtmɔnɛ]
safe	**coffre fort** (m)	[kɔfr fɔr]
heir	**héritier** (m)	[eritje]
inheritance	**héritage** (m)	[eritaʒ]
fortune (wealth)	**fortune** (f)	[fɔrtyn]
lease, rent	**location** (f)	[lɔkasjɔ̃]
rent money	**loyer** (m)	[lwaje]
to rent (sth from sb)	**louer** (vt)	[lwe]
price	**prix** (m)	[pri]
cost	**coût** (m)	[ku]
sum	**somme** (f)	[sɔm]
to spend (vt)	**dépenser** (vt)	[depɑ̃se]
expenses	**dépenses** (f pl)	[depɑ̃s]
to economize (vi, vt)	**économiser** (vt)	[ekɔnɔmize]
economical	**économe** (adj)	[ekɔnɔm]
to pay (vi, vt)	**payer** (vi, vt)	[peje]
payment	**paiement** (m)	[pɛmɑ̃]
change (give the ~)	**monnaie** (f)	[mɔnɛ]
tax	**impôt** (m)	[ɛ̃po]
fine	**amende** (f)	[amɑ̃d]
to fine (vt)	**mettre une amende**	[mɛtr ynamɑ̃d]

60. Post. Postal service

post office	**poste** (f)	[pɔst]
mail (letters, etc.)	**courrier** (m)	[kurje]
mailman	**facteur** (m)	[faktœr]
opening hours	**heures** (f pl) **d'ouverture**	[zœr duvɛrtyr]
letter	**lettre** (f)	[lɛtr]
registered letter	**recommandé** (m)	[rəkɔmɑ̃de]
postcard	**carte** (f) **postale**	[kart pɔstal]
telegram	**télégramme** (m)	[telegram]
parcel	**colis** (m)	[kɔli]
money transfer	**mandat** (m) **postal**	[mɑ̃da pɔstal]
to receive (vt)	**recevoir** (vt)	[rəsəvwar]
to send (vt)	**envoyer** (vt)	[ɑ̃vwaje]
sending	**envoi** (m)	[ɑ̃vwa]
address	**adresse** (f)	[adrɛs]
ZIP code	**code** (m) **postal**	[kɔd pɔstal]
sender	**expéditeur** (m)	[ɛkspeditœr]
receiver, addressee	**destinataire** (m)	[dɛstinatɛr]
name	**prénom** (m)	[prenɔ̃]
family name	**nom** (m) **de famille**	[nɔ̃ də famij]
rate (of postage)	**tarif** (m)	[tarif]
standard (adj)	**normal** (adj)	[nɔrmal]
economical (adj)	**économique** (adj)	[ekɔnɔmik]
weight	**poids** (m)	[pwa]
to weigh up (vt)	**peser** (vt)	[pəze]
envelope	**enveloppe** (f)	[ɑ̃vlɔp]
postage stamp	**timbre** (m)	[tɛ̃br]
to stamp an envelope	**timbrer** (vt)	[tɛ̃bre]

Dwelling. House. Home

61. House. Electricity

electricity	électricité (f)	[elɛktrisite]
light bulb	ampoule (f)	[ɑ̃pul]
switch	interrupteur (m)	[ɛ̃teryptœr]
fuse	plomb, fusible (m)	[plɔ̃], [fyzibl]
cable, wire (electric ~)	fil (m)	[fil]
wiring	installation (f) électrique	[ɛ̃stalasjɔ̃ elɛktrik]
electricity meter	compteur (m) électrique	[kɔ̃tœr elɛktrik]
readings	relevé (m)	[rəlve]

62. Villa. Mansion

country house	maison (f) de campagne	[mɛzɔ̃ də kɑ̃paɲ]
villa (by sea)	villa (f)	[vila]
wing (of building)	aile (f)	[ɛl]
garden	jardin (m)	[ʒardɛ̃]
park	parc (m)	[park]
tropical greenhouse	serre (f) tropicale	[sɛr trɔpikal]
to look after (garden, etc.)	s'occuper de ...	[sɔkype də]
swimming pool	piscine (f)	[pisin]
gym	salle (f) de gym	[sal də ʒim]
tennis court	court (m) de tennis	[kur də tenis]
home theater room	salle (f) de cinéma	[sal də sinema]
garage	garage (m)	[garaʒ]
private property	propriété (f) privée	[prɔprijete prive]
private land	terrain (m) privé	[tɛrɛ̃ prive]
warning (caution)	avertissement (m)	[avɛrtismɑ̃]
warning sign	panneau (m) d'avertissement	[pano davɛrtismɑ̃]
security	sécurité (f)	[sekyrite]
security guard	agent (m) de sécurité	[aʒɑ̃ də sekyrite]
burglar alarm	alarme (f) antivol	[alarm ɑ̃tivɔl]

63. Apartment

apartment	appartement (m)	[apartəmɑ̃]
room	chambre (f)	[ʃɑ̃br]
bedroom	chambre (f) à coucher	[ʃɑ̃br a kuʃe]
dining room	salle (f) à manger	[sal a mɑ̃ʒe]
living room	salon (m)	[salɔ̃]
study (home office)	bureau (m)	[byro]
entry room	antichambre (f)	[ɑ̃tiʃɑ̃br]
bathroom	salle (f) de bains	[sal də bɛ̃]
half bath	toilettes (f pl)	[twalɛt]
ceiling	plafond (m)	[plafɔ̃]
floor	plancher (m)	[plɑ̃ʃe]
corner	coin (m)	[kwɛ̃]

64. Furniture. Interior

furniture	meubles (m pl)	[mœbl]
table	table (f)	[tabl]
chair	chaise (f)	[ʃɛz]
bed	lit (m)	[li]
couch, sofa	canapé (m)	[kanape]
armchair	fauteuil (m)	[fotœj]
bookcase	bibliothèque (f)	[biblijɔtɛk]
shelf	rayon (m)	[rɛjɔ̃]
set of shelves	étagère (f)	[etaʒɛr]
wardrobe	armoire (f)	[armwar]
coat rack	patère (f)	[patɛr]
coat stand	portemanteau (m)	[pɔrtmɑ̃to]
dresser	commode (f)	[kɔmɔd]
coffee table	table (f) basse	[tabl bas]
mirror	miroir (m)	[mirwar]
carpet	tapis (m)	[tapi]
rug, small carpet	petit tapis (m)	[pəti tapi]
fireplace	cheminée (f)	[ʃəmine]
candle	bougie (f)	[buʒi]
candlestick	chandelier (m)	[ʃɑ̃dəlje]
drapes	rideaux (m pl)	[rido]
wallpaper	papier (m) peint	[papje pɛ̃]
blinds (jalousie)	jalousie (f)	[ʒaluzi]
table lamp	lampe (f) de table	[lɑ̃p də tabl]

wall lamp (sconce)	**applique** (f)	[aplik]
floor lamp	**lampadaire** (m)	[lɑ̃padɛr]
chandelier	**lustre** (m)	[lystr]

leg (of chair, table)	**pied** (m)	[pje]
armrest	**accoudoir** (m)	[akudwar]
back (backrest)	**dossier** (m)	[dosje]
drawer	**tiroir** (m)	[tirwar]

65. Bedding

bedclothes	**linge** (m) **de lit**	[lɛ̃ʒ də li]
pillow	**oreiller** (m)	[ɔrɛje]
pillowcase	**taie** (f) **d'oreiller**	[tɛ dɔrɛje]
blanket (comforter)	**couverture** (f)	[kuvɛrtyr]
sheet	**drap** (m)	[dra]
bedspread	**couvre-lit** (m)	[kuvrəli]

66. Kitchen

kitchen	**cuisine** (f)	[kɥizin]
gas	**gaz** (m)	[gaz]
gas cooker	**cuisinière** (f) **à gaz**	[kɥizinjɛr ɑ gaz]
electric cooker	**cuisinière** (f) **électrique**	[kɥizinjɛr elɛktrik]
oven	**four** (m)	[fur]
microwave oven	**four** (m) **micro-ondes**	[fur mikrɔɔ̃d]

refrigerator	**réfrigérateur** (m)	[refriʒeratœr]
freezer	**congélateur** (m)	[kɔ̃ʒelatœr]
dishwasher	**lave-vaisselle** (m)	[lavvesɛl]

meat grinder	**hachoir** (m)	[aʃwar]
juicer	**centrifugeuse** (f)	[sɑ̃trifyʒøz]
toaster	**grille-pain** (m)	[grijpɛ̃]
mixer	**batteur** (m)	[batœr]

coffee maker	**machine** (f) **à café**	[maʃin ɑ kafe]
coffee pot	**cafetière** (f)	[kaftjɛr]
coffee grinder	**moulin** (m) **à café**	[mulɛ̃ ɑ kafe]

kettle	**bouilloire** (f)	[bujwar]
teapot	**théière** (f)	[tejɛr]
lid	**couvercle** (m)	[kuvɛrkl]
tea strainer	**passoire** (f) **à thé**	[pɑswar ɑ te]

spoon	**cuillère** (f)	[kɥijɛr]
teaspoon	**petite cuillère** (f)	[pətit kɥijɛr]
tablespoon	**cuillère** (f) **à soupe**	[kɥijɛr ɑ sup]

| fork | fourchette (f) | [furʃɛt] |
| knife | couteau (m) | [kuto] |

tableware (dishes)	vaisselle (f)	[vɛsɛl]
plate (dinner ~)	assiette (f)	[asjɛt]
saucer	soucoupe (f)	[sukup]

shot glass	verre (m) à shot	[vɛr ɑ ʃot]
glass (~ of water)	verre (m)	[vɛr]
cup	tasse (f)	[tɑs]

sugar bowl	sucrier (m)	[sykrije]
salt shaker	salière (f)	[saljɛr]
pepper shaker	poivrière (f)	[pwavrijɛr]
butter dish	beurrier (m)	[bœrje]

saucepan	casserole (f)	[kasrɔl]
frying pan	poêle (f)	[pwal]
ladle	louche (f)	[luʃ]
colander	passoire (f)	[pɑswar]
tray	plateau (m)	[plato]

bottle	bouteille (f)	[butɛj]
jar (glass)	bocal (m)	[bɔkal]
can	boîte (f) en fer-blanc	[bwat ɑ̃ fɛrblɑ̃]

bottle opener	ouvre-bouteille (m)	[uvrəbutɛj]
can opener	ouvre-boîte (m)	[uvrəbwat]
corkscrew	tire-bouchon (m)	[tirbuʃɔ̃]
filter	filtre (m)	[filtr]
to filter (vt)	filtrer (vt)	[filtre]

| trash | ordures (f pl) | [ɔrdyr] |
| trash can | poubelle (f) | [pubɛl] |

67. Bathroom

bathroom	salle (f) de bains	[sal də bɛ̃]
water	eau (f)	[o]
tap, faucet	robinet (m)	[rɔbinɛ]
hot water	eau (f) chaude	[o ʃod]
cold water	eau (f) froide	[o frwad]

toothpaste	dentifrice (m)	[dɑ̃tifris]
to brush one's teeth	se brosser les dents	[sə brɔse le dɑ̃]
toothbrush	brosse (f) à dents	[brɔs ɑ dɑ̃]

to shave (vi)	se raser (vp)	[sə raze]
shaving foam	mousse (f) à raser	[mus ɑ raze]
razor	rasoir (m)	[razwar]

to wash (one's hands, etc.)	laver (vt)	[lave]
to take a bath	se laver (vp)	[sə lave]
shower	douche (f)	[duʃ]
to take a shower	prendre une douche	[prɑ̃dr yn duʃ]

bathtub	baignoire (f)	[bɛɲwar]
toilet (toilet bowl)	cuvette (f)	[kyvɛt]
sink (washbasin)	lavabo (m)	[lavabo]

soap	savon (m)	[savɔ̃]
soap dish	porte-savon (m)	[pɔrtsavɔ̃]

sponge	éponge (f)	[epɔ̃ʒ]
shampoo	shampooing (m)	[ʃɑ̃pwɛ̃]
towel	serviette (f)	[sɛrvjɛt]
bathrobe	peignoir (m) de bain	[pɛɲwar də bɛ̃]

laundry (process)	lessive (f)	[lɛsiv]
washing machine	machine (f) à laver	[maʃin a lave]
to do the laundry	faire la lessive	[fɛr la lɛsiv]
laundry detergent	lessive (f)	[lɛsiv]

68. Household appliances

TV set	télé (f)	[tele]
tape recorder	magnétophone (m)	[maɲetɔfɔn]
video, VCR	magnétoscope (m)	[maɲetɔskɔp]
radio	radio (f)	[radjo]
player (CD, MP3, etc.)	lecteur (m)	[lɛktœr]

video projector	vidéoprojecteur (m)	[videoprɔʒɛktœr]
home movie theater	home cinéma (m)	[həʊm sinema]
DVD player	lecteur DVD (m)	[lɛktœr devede]
amplifier	amplificateur (m)	[ɑ̃plifikatœr]
video game console	console (f) de jeux	[kɔ̃sɔl də ʒø]

video camera	caméscope (m)	[kameskɔp]
camera (photo)	appareil (m) photo	[aparɛj fɔto]
digital camera	appareil (m) photo numérique	[aparɛj fɔto nymerik]

vacuum cleaner	aspirateur (m)	[aspiratœr]
iron (e.g., steam ~)	fer (m) à repasser	[fɛr a rəpase]
ironing board	planche (f) à repasser	[plɑ̃ʃ a rəpase]

telephone	téléphone (m)	[telefɔn]
mobile phone	portable (m)	[pɔrtabl]
typewriter	machine (f) à écrire	[maʃin a ekrir]
sewing machine	machine (f) à coudre	[maʃin a kudr]
microphone	micro (m)	[mikro]

| headphones | écouteurs (m pl) | [ekutœr] |
| remote control (TV) | télécommande (f) | [telekɔmɑ̃d] |

CD, compact disc	CD (m)	[sede]
cassette	cassette (f)	[kasɛt]
vinyl record	disque (m) vinyle	[disk vinil]

HUMAN ACTIVITIES

Job. Business. Part 1

69. Office. Working in the office

office (of firm)	**bureau** (m)	[byro]
office (of director, etc.)	**bureau** (m)	[byro]
front desk	**accueil** (m)	[akœj]
secretary	**secrétaire** (m)	[səkretɛr]
secretary (fem.)	**secrétaire** (f)	[səkretɛr]
director	**directeur** (m)	[dirɛktœr]
manager	**manager** (m)	[manadʒœr]
accountant	**comptable** (m)	[kɔ̃tabl]
employee	**collaborateur** (m)	[kɔlabɔratœr]
furniture	**meubles** (m pl)	[mœbl]
desk	**bureau** (m)	[byro]
desk chair	**fauteuil** (m)	[fotœj]
chest of drawers	**classeur** (m) **à tiroirs**	[klasœr a tirwar]
coat stand	**portemanteau** (m)	[pɔrtmɑ̃to]
computer	**ordinateur** (m)	[ɔrdinatœr]
printer	**imprimante** (f)	[ɛ̃primɑ̃t]
fax machine	**fax** (m)	[faks]
photocopier	**copieuse** (f)	[kɔpjøz]
paper	**papier** (m)	[papje]
office supplies	**papeterie** (f)	[papɛtri]
mouse pad	**tapis** (m) **de souris**	[tapi də suri]
sheet (of paper)	**feuille** (f)	[fœj]
folder, binder	**classeur** (m)	[klasœr]
catalog	**catalogue** (m)	[katalɔg]
phone book (directory)	**annuaire** (m)	[anɥɛr]
documentation	**documents** (m pl)	[dɔkymɑ̃]
brochure	**brochure** (f)	[brɔʃyr]
(e.g., 12 pages ~)		
leaflet	**prospectus** (m)	[prɔspɛktys]
sample	**échantillon** (m)	[eʃɑ̃tijɔ̃]
training meeting	**formation** (f)	[fɔrmasjɔ̃]
meeting (of managers)	**réunion** (f)	[reynjɔ̃]
lunch time	**pause** (f) **déjeuner**	[poz deʒœne]

to make a copy	faire une copie	[fɛr yn kɔpi]
to make copies	faire des copies	[fɛr de kɔpi]
to receive a fax	recevoir un fax	[rəsəvwar œ̃ faks]
to send a fax	envoyer un fax	[ɑ̃vwaje œ̃ faks]

to call (by phone)	téléphoner, appeler	[telefɔne], [aple]
to answer (vt)	répondre (vi, vt)	[repɔ̃dr]
to put through	passer (vt)	[pɑse]

to arrange, to set up	fixer (vt)	[fikse]
to demonstrate (vt)	montrer (vt)	[mɔ̃tre]
to be absent	être absent	[ɛtr apsɑ̃]
absence	absence (f)	[apsɑ̃s]

70. Business processes. Part 1

| business | affaire (f) | [afɛr] |
| occupation | métier (m) | [metje] |

firm	firme (f), société (f)	[firm], [sɔsjete]
company	compagnie (f)	[kɔ̃paɲi]
corporation	corporation (f)	[kɔrpɔrasjɔ̃]
enterprise	entreprise (f)	[ɑ̃trœpriz]
agency	agence (f)	[aʒɑ̃s]

agreement (contract)	accord (m)	[akɔr]
contract	contrat (m)	[kɔ̃tra]
deal	marché (m)	[marʃe]
order (to place an ~)	commande (f)	[kɔmɑ̃d]
term (of contract)	terme (m)	[tɛrm]

wholesale (adv)	en gros (adv)	[ɑ̃ gro]
wholesale (adj)	en gros (adj)	[ɑ̃ gro]
wholesale (n)	vente (f) en gros	[vɑ̃t ɑ̃ gro]
retail (adj)	au détail (adj)	[odetaj]
retail (n)	vente (f) au détail	[vɑ̃t o detaj]

competitor	concurrent (m)	[kɔ̃kyrɑ̃]
competition	concurrence (f)	[kɔ̃kyrɑ̃s]
to compete (vi)	concurrencer (vt)	[kɔ̃kyrɑ̃se]

| partner (associate) | associé (m) | [asɔsje] |
| partnership | partenariat (m) | [partənarja] |

crisis	crise (f)	[kriz]
bankruptcy	faillite (f)	[fajit]
to go bankrupt	faire faillite	[fɛr fajit]
difficulty	difficulté (f)	[difikylte]
problem	problème (m)	[prɔblɛm]
catastrophe	catastrophe (f)	[katastrɔf]

economy	économie (f)	[ekɔnɔmi]
economic (~ growth)	économique (adj)	[ekɔnɔmik]
economic recession	baisse (f) économique	[bɛs ekɔnɔmik]

goal (aim)	but (m)	[byt]
task	objectif (m)	[ɔbʒɛktif]

to trade (vi)	faire du commerce	[fɛr dy kɔmɛrs]
network (distribution ~)	réseau (m)	[rezo]
inventory (stock)	inventaire (m)	[ɛ̃vɑ̃tɛr]
assortment	assortiment (m)	[asɔrtimɑ̃]

leader (leading company)	leader (m)	[lidœr]
large (~ company)	grand, grande (adj)	[grɑ̃, grɑ̃d]
monopoly	monopole (m)	[mɔnɔpɔl]

theory	théorie (f)	[teɔri]
practice	pratique (f)	[pratik]
experience (in my ~)	expérience (f)	[ɛksperjɑ̃s]
trend (tendency)	tendance (f)	[tɑ̃dɑ̃s]
development	développement (m)	[devlɔpmɑ̃]

71. Business processes. Part 2

benefit, profit	rentabilité (m)	[rɑ̃tabilite]
profitable (adj)	rentable (adj)	[rɑ̃tabl]

delegation (group)	délégation (f)	[delegasjɔ̃]
salary	salaire (m)	[salɛr]
to correct (an error)	corriger (vt)	[kɔriʒe]
business trip	voyage (m) d'affaires	[vwajaʒ dafɛr]
commission	commission (f)	[kɔmisjɔ̃]

to control (vt)	contrôler (vt)	[kɔ̃trole]
conference	conférence (f)	[kɔ̃ferɑ̃s]
license	licence (f)	[lisɑ̃s]
reliable (~ partner)	fiable (adj)	[fjabl]

initiative (undertaking)	initiative (f)	[inisjativ]
norm (standard)	norme (f)	[nɔrm]
circumstance	circonstance (f)	[sirkɔ̃stɑ̃s]
duty (of employee)	fonction (f)	[fɔ̃ksjɔ̃]

organization (company)	entreprise (f)	[ɑ̃trœpriz]
organization (process)	organisation (f)	[ɔrganizasjɔ̃]
organized (adj)	organisé (adj)	[ɔrganize]
cancellation	annulation (f)	[anylasjɔ̃]
to cancel (call off)	annuler (vt)	[anyle]
report (official ~)	rapport (m)	[rapɔr]
patent	brevet (m)	[brəvɛ]

to patent (obtain patent)	breveter (vt)	[brəvte]
to plan (vt)	planifier (vt)	[planifje]

bonus (money)	prime (f)	[prim]
professional (adj)	professionnel (adj)	[prɔfɛsjɔnɛl]
procedure	procédure (f)	[prɔsedyr]

to examine (contract, etc.)	examiner (vt)	[ɛgzamine]
calculation	calcul (m)	[kalkyl]
reputation	réputation (f)	[repytasjɔ̃]
risk	risque (m)	[risk]

to manage, to run	diriger (vt)	[diriʒe]
information	renseignements (m pl)	[rɑ̃sɛɲəmɑ̃]
property	propriété (f)	[prɔprijete]
union	union (f)	[ynjɔ̃]

life insurance	assurance vie (f)	[asyrɑ̃s vi]
to insure (vt)	assurer (vt)	[asyre]
insurance	assurance (f)	[asyrɑ̃s]

auction (~ sale)	enchères (f pl)	[ɑ̃ʃɛr]
to notify (inform)	notifier (vt)	[nɔtifje]
management (process)	gestion (f)	[ʒɛstjɔ̃]
service (~ industry)	service (m)	[sɛrvis]

forum	forum (m)	[fɔrɔm]
to function (vi)	fonctionner (vi)	[fɔ̃ksjɔne]
stage (phase)	étape (f)	[etap]
legal (~ services)	juridique (adj)	[ʒyridik]
lawyer (legal expert)	juriste (m)	[ʒyrist]

72. Production. Works

plant	usine (f)	[yzin]
factory	fabrique (f)	[fabrik]
workshop	atelier (m)	[atəlje]
works, production site	site (m) de production	[sit də prɔdyksjɔ̃]

industry	industrie (f)	[ɛ̃dystri]
industrial (adj)	industriel (adj)	[ɛ̃dystrijɛl]
heavy industry	industrie (f) lourde	[ɛ̃dystri lurd]
light industry	industrie (f) légère	[ɛ̃dystri leʒɛr]

products	produit (m)	[prɔdyi]
to produce (vt)	produire (vt)	[prɔdɥir]
raw materials	matières (f pl) premières	[matjɛr prəmjɛr]

foreman	chef (m) d'équipe	[ʃɛf dekip]
workers team	équipe (f) d'ouvriers	[ekip duvrije]

worker	ouvrier (m)	[uvrije]
working day	jour (m) ouvrable	[ʒur uvrabl]
pause	pause (f)	[poz]
meeting	réunion (f)	[reynjõ]
to discuss (vt)	discuter (vt)	[diskyte]

plan	plan (m)	[plã]
to fulfill the plan	accomplir le plan	[akõplir lə plã]
rate of output	norme (f) de production	[nɔrm də prɔdyksjõ]
quality	qualité (f)	[kalite]
checking (control)	contrôle (m)	[kõtrol]
quality control	contrôle (m) qualité	[kõtrol kalite]

work safety	sécurité (f) de travail	[sekyrite də travaj]
discipline	discipline (f)	[disiplin]
violation	infraction (f)	[ɛ̃fraksjõ]
(of safety rules, etc.)		
to violate (rules)	violer (vt)	[vjɔle]
strike	grève (f)	[grɛv]
striker	gréviste (m)	[grevist]
to be on strike	faire grève	[fɛr grɛv]
labor union	syndicat (m)	[sɛ̃dika]

to invent (machine, etc.)	inventer (vt)	[ɛ̃vãte]
invention	invention (f)	[ɛ̃vãsjõ]
research	recherche (f)	[rəʃɛrʃ]
to improve (make better)	améliorer (vt)	[ameljɔre]
technology	technologie (f)	[tɛknɔlɔʒi]
technical drawing	dessin (m) technique	[desɛ̃ tɛknik]

load, cargo	charge (f)	[ʃarʒ]
loader (person)	chargeur (m)	[ʃarʒœr]
to load (vehicle, etc.)	charger (vt)	[ʃarʒe]
loading (process)	chargement (m)	[ʃarʒəmã]
to unload (vi, vt)	décharger (vt)	[deʃarʒe]
unloading	déchargement (m)	[deʃarʒəmã]

transportation	transport (m)	[trãspɔr]
transportation company	compagnie (f) de transport	[kõpaɲi də trãspɔr]
to transport (vt)	transporter (vt)	[trãspɔrte]

freight car	wagon de marchandise	[vagõ də marʃãdiz]
cistern	citerne (f)	[sitɛrn]
truck	camion (m)	[kamjõ]

machine tool	machine-outil (f)	[maʃinuti]
mechanism	mécanisme (m)	[mekanism]

industrial waste	déchets (m pl)	[deʃɛ]
packing (process)	emballage (m)	[ãbalaʒ]
to pack (vt)	emballer (vt)	[ãbale]

73. Contract. Agreement

contract	**contrat** (m)	[kɔ̃tra]
agreement	**accord** (m)	[akɔr]
addendum	**annexe** (f)	[anɛks]
to sign a contract	**signer un contrat**	[siɲe œ̃ kɔ̃tra]
signature	**signature** (f)	[siɲatyr]
to sign (vt)	**signer** (vt)	[siɲe]
stamp (seal)	**cachet** (m)	[kaʃe]
subject of contract	**objet** (m) **du contrat**	[ɔbʒɛ dy kɔ̃tra]
clause	**clause** (f)	[kloz]
parties (in contract)	**côtés** (m pl)	[kote]
legal address	**adresse** (f) **légale**	[adrɛs legal]
to break the contract	**violer l'accord**	[vjole lakɔr]
commitment	**obligation** (f)	[ɔbligasjɔ̃]
responsibility	**responsabilité** (f)	[rɛspɔ̃sabilite]
force majeure	**force** (f) **majeure**	[fɔrs maʒœr]
dispute	**litige** (m)	[litiʒ]
penalties	**pénalités** (f pl)	[penalite]

74. Import & Export

import	**importation** (f)	[ɛ̃pɔrtasjɔ̃]
importer	**importateur** (m)	[ɛ̃pɔrtatœr]
to import (vt)	**importer** (vt)	[ɛ̃pɔrte]
import (e.g., ~ goods)	**d'importation**	[dɛ̃pɔrtasjɔ̃]
export	**exportation** (f)	[ɛkspɔrtasjɔ̃]
exporter	**exportateur** (m)	[ɛkspɔrtatœr]
to export (vi, vt)	**exporter** (vt)	[ɛkspɔrte]
export (e.g., ~ goods)	**à l'export**	[a lɛkspɔr]
goods	**marchandise** (f)	[marʃɑ̃diz]
consignment, lot	**lot** (m) **de marchandises**	[lo də marʃɑ̃diz]
weight	**poids** (m)	[pwa]
volume	**volume** (m)	[vɔlym]
cubic meter	**mètre** (m) **cube**	[mɛtr kyb]
manufacturer	**producteur** (m)	[prɔdyktœr]
transportation company	**compagnie** (f) **de transport**	[kɔ̃paɲi də trɑ̃spɔr]
container	**container** (m)	[kɔ̃tɛnɛr]
border	**frontière** (f)	[frɔ̃tjɛr]
customs	**douane** (f)	[dwan]

customs duty	droit (m) de douane	[drwa də dwan]
customs officer	douanier (m)	[dwanje]
smuggling	contrebande (f)	[kɔ̃trəbɑ̃d]
contraband (goods)	contrebande (f)	[kɔ̃trəbɑ̃d]

75. Finances

stock (share)	action (f)	[aksjɔ̃]
bond (certificate)	obligation (f)	[ɔbligasjɔ̃]
bill of exchange	lettre (f) de change	[lɛtr də ʃɑ̃ʒ]

stock exchange	bourse (f)	[burs]
stock price	cours (m) d'actions	[kur daksjɔ̃]

to go down	baisser (vi)	[bese]
to go up	augmenter (vi)	[ogmɑ̃te]

shareholding	part (f)	[par]
controlling interest	participation (f) de contrôle	[partisipasjɔ̃ də kɔ̃trol]

investment	investissements (m pl)	[ɛ̃vɛstismɑ̃]
to invest (vt)	investir (vt)	[ɛ̃vɛstir]
percent	pour-cent (m)	[pursɑ̃]
interest (on investment)	intérêts (m pl)	[ɛ̃terɛ]
profit	profit (m)	[prɔfi]
profitable (adj)	profitable (adj)	[prɔfitabl]
tax	impôt (m)	[ɛ̃po]

currency (foreign ~)	devise (f)	[dəviz]
national (adj)	national (adj)	[nasjɔnal]
exchange (currency ~)	échange (m)	[eʃɑ̃ʒ]

accountant	comptable (m)	[kɔ̃tabl]
accounting	comptabilité (f)	[kɔ̃tabilite]

bankruptcy	faillite (f)	[fajit]
collapse, crash	krach (m)	[krak]
ruin	ruine (f)	[rɥin]
to be ruined	se ruiner (vp)	[sə rɥine]
inflation	inflation (f)	[ɛ̃flasjɔ̃]
devaluation	dévaluation (f)	[devalɥasjɔ̃]

capital	capital (m)	[kapital]
income	revenu (m)	[rəvəny]
turnover	chiffre (m) d'affaires	[ʃifr dafɛr]
resources	ressources (f pl)	[rəsurs]
monetary resources	moyens (m pl) financiers	[mwajɛ̃ finɑ̃sje]
overhead	frais (m pl) généraux	[frɛ ʒenerø]
to reduce (expenses)	réduire (vt)	[redɥir]

76. Marketing

marketing	marketing (m)	[marketin]
market	marché (m)	[marʃe]
market segment	segment (m) du marché	[sɛgmã dy marʃe]
product	produit (m)	[prɔdyi]
goods	marchandise (f)	[marʃãdiz]
brand	marque (f) de fabrique	[mark də fabrik]
trademark	marque (f) déposée	[mark depoze]
logotype	logotype (m)	[lɔgɔtip]
logo	logo (m)	[logo]
demand	demande (f)	[dəmãd]
supply	offre (f)	[ɔfr]
need	besoin (m)	[bəzwɛ̃]
consumer	consommateur (m)	[kɔ̃sɔmatœr]
analysis	analyse (f)	[analiz]
to analyze (vt)	analyser (vt)	[analize]
positioning	positionnement (m)	[pozisjɔnmã]
to position (vt)	positionner (vt)	[pozisjɔne]
price	prix (m)	[pri]
pricing policy	politique (f) des prix	[pɔlitik de pri]
formation of price	formation (f) des prix	[fɔrmasjɔ̃ de pri]

77. Advertising

advertising	publicité (f), pub (f)	[pyblisite], [pyb]
to advertise (vt)	faire de la publicité	[fɛr də la pyblisite]
budget	budget (m)	[bydʒɛ]
ad, advertisement	annonce (f), pub (f)	[anɔ̃s], [pyb]
TV advertising	publicité (f) à la télévision	[pyblisite ɑla televizjɔ̃]
radio advertising	publicité (f) à la radio	[pyblisite ɑla radjo]
outdoor advertising	publicité (f) extérieure	[pyblisite ɛksterjœr]
mass media	mass média (m pl)	[masmedja]
periodical (n)	périodique (m)	[perjɔdik]
image (public appearance)	image (f)	[imaʒ]
slogan	slogan (m)	[slɔgã]
motto (maxim)	devise (f)	[dəviz]
campaign	campagne (f)	[kãpaɲ]
advertising campaign	campagne (f) publicitaire	[kãpaɲ pyblisitɛr]
target group	public (m) cible	[pyblik sibl]

85

business card	carte (f) de visite	[kart də vizit]
leaflet	prospectus (m)	[prɔspɛktys]
brochure	brochure (f)	[brɔʃyr]
(e.g., 12 pages ~)		
pamphlet	dépliant (m)	[deplijã]
newsletter	bulletin (m)	[byltɛ̃]
store sign	enseigne (f)	[ãsɛɲ]
poster	poster (m)	[pɔstɛr]
billboard	panneau-réclame (m)	[pano reklam]

78. Banking

bank	banque (f)	[bãk]
branch (of bank, etc.)	agence (f) bancaire	[aʒãs bãkɛr]
bank clerk, consultant	conseiller (m)	[kõseje]
manager (director)	gérant (m)	[ʒerã]
banking account	compte (m)	[kõt]
account number	numéro (m) du compte	[nymero dy kõt]
checking account	compte (m) courant	[kõt kurã]
savings account	compte (m) sur livret	[kõt syr livrɛ]
to open an account	ouvrir un compte	[uvrir œ̃ kõt]
to close the account	clôturer le compte	[klotyre lə kõt]
to deposit into the account	verser dans le compte	[vɛrse dã lə kõt]
to withdraw (vt)	retirer du compte	[rətire dy kõt]
deposit	dépôt (m)	[depo]
to make a deposit	faire un dépôt	[fɛr œ̃ depo]
wire transfer	virement (m) bancaire	[virmã bãkɛr]
to wire, to transfer	faire un transfert	[fɛr œ̃ trãsfɛr]
sum	somme (f)	[sɔm]
How much?	Combien?	[kõbjɛ̃]
signature	signature (f)	[siɲatyr]
to sign (vt)	signer (vt)	[siɲe]
credit card	carte (f) de crédit	[kart də kredi]
code	code (m)	[kɔd]
credit card number	numéro (m) de carte de crédit	[nymero də kart də kredi]
ATM	distributeur (m)	[distribytœr]
check	chèque (m)	[ʃɛk]
to write a check	faire un chèque	[fɛr œ̃ ʃɛk]
checkbook	chéquier (m)	[ʃekje]
loan (bank ~)	crédit (m)	[kredi]

to apply for a loan	demander un crédit	[dəmɑ̃de œ̃ kredi]
to get a loan	prendre un crédit	[prɑ̃dr œ̃ kredi]
to give a loan	accorder un crédit	[akɔrde œ̃ kredi]
guarantee	gage (m)	[gaʒ]

79. Telephone. Phone conversation

telephone	téléphone (m)	[telefɔn]
mobile phone	portable (m)	[pɔrtabl]
answering machine	répondeur (m)	[repɔ̃dœr]

| to call (telephone) | téléphoner, appeler | [telefɔne], [aple] |
| phone call | appel (m) | [apɛl] |

to dial a number	composer le numéro	[kɔ̃poze lə nymero]
Hello!	Allô!	[alo]
to ask (vt)	demander (vt)	[dəmɑ̃de]
to answer (vi, vt)	répondre (vi, vt)	[repɔ̃dr]

to hear (vt)	entendre (vt)	[ɑ̃tɑ̃dr]
well (adv)	bien (adv)	[bjɛ̃]
not well (adv)	mal (adv)	[mal]
noises (interference)	bruits (m pl)	[brɥi]

receiver	récepteur (m)	[resɛptœr]
to pick up (~ the phone)	décrocher (vt)	[dekrɔʃe]
to hang up (~ the phone)	raccrocher (vi)	[rakrɔʃe]

busy (adj)	occupé (adj)	[ɔkype]
to ring (ab. phone)	sonner (vi)	[sɔ̃]
telephone book	carnet (m) de téléphone	[karnɛ də telefɔn]

local (adj)	local (adj)	[lɔkal]
local call	appel (m) local	[apɛl lɔkal]
long distance (~ call)	interurbain (adj)	[ɛ̃tɛryrbɛ̃]
long-distance call	appel (m) interurbain	[apɛl ɛ̃tɛryrbɛ̃]
international (adj)	international (adj)	[ɛ̃tɛrnasjɔnal]
international call	appel (m) international	[apɛl ɛ̃tɛrnasjɔnal]

80. Mobile telephone

mobile phone	portable (m)	[pɔrtabl]
display	écran (m)	[ekrɑ̃]
button	bouton (m)	[butɔ̃]
SIM card	carte SIM (f)	[kart sim]

| battery | pile (f) | [pil] |
| to be dead (battery) | être déchargé | [ɛtr deʃarʒe] |

charger	chargeur (m)	[ʃarʒœr]
menu	menu (m)	[məny]
settings	réglages (m pl)	[reglaʒ]
tune (melody)	mélodie (f)	[melɔdi]
to select (vt)	sélectionner (vt)	[selɛksjɔne]

calculator	calculatrice (f)	[kalkylatris]
voice mail	répondeur (m)	[repɔ̃dœr]
alarm clock	réveil (m)	[revɛj]
contacts	contacts (m pl)	[kɔ̃takt]

| SMS (text message) | SMS (m) | [esemes] |
| subscriber | abonné (m) | [abɔne] |

81. Stationery

| ballpoint pen | stylo (m) à bille | [stilo a bij] |
| fountain pen | stylo (m) à plume | [stilo a plym] |

pencil	crayon (m)	[krɛjɔ̃]
highlighter	marqueur (m)	[markœr]
felt-tip pen	feutre (m)	[føtr]

| notepad | bloc-notes (m) | [blɔknɔt] |
| agenda (diary) | agenda (m) | [aʒɛ̃da] |

| ruler | règle (f) | [rɛgl] |
| calculator | calculatrice (f) | [kalkylatris] |

eraser	gomme (f)	[gɔm]
thumbtack	punaise (f)	[pynɛz]
paper clip	trombone (m)	[trɔ̃bɔn]

glue	colle (f)	[kɔl]
stapler	agrafeuse (f)	[agraføz]
hole punch	perforateur (m)	[pɛrfɔratœr]
pencil sharpener	taille-crayon (m)	[tajkrɛjɔ̃]

82. Kinds of business

accounting services	services (m pl) comptables	[sɛrvis kɔ̃tabl]
advertising	publicité (f), pub (f)	[pyblisite], [pyb]
advertising agency	agence (f) publicitaire	[aʒɑ̃s pyblisitɛr]
air-conditioners	climatisation (m)	[klimatizasjɔ̃]
airline	compagnie (f) aérienne	[kɔ̃paɲi aerjɛn]
alcoholic drinks	boissons (f pl) alcoolisées	[bwasɔ̃ alkɔlize]

antiquities	**antiquités** (f pl)	[ɑ̃tikite]
art gallery	**galerie** (f) **d'art**	[galri dar]
audit services	**services** (m pl) **d'audition**	[sɛrvis dodisjɔ̃]
banks	**banques** (f pl)	[bɑ̃k]
bar	**bar** (m)	[bar]
beauty parlor	**salon** (m) **de beauté**	[salɔ̃ də bote]
bookstore	**librairie** (f)	[librɛri]
brewery	**brasserie** (f)	[brasri]
business center	**centre** (m) **d'affaires**	[sɑ̃tr dafɛr]
business school	**école** (f) **de commerce**	[ekɔl də kɔmɛrs]
casino	**casino** (m)	[kazino]
construction	**bâtiment** (m)	[batimɑ̃]
consulting	**conseil** (m)	[kɔ̃sɛj]
dental clinic	**dentistes** (pl)	[dɑ̃tists]
design	**design** (m)	[dizajn]
drugstore, pharmacy	**pharmacie** (f)	[farmasi]
dry cleaners	**pressing** (m)	[presiŋ]
employment agency	**agence** (f) **de recrutement**	[aʒɑ̃s də rəkrytmɑ̃]
financial services	**service** (m) **financier**	[sɛrvis finɑ̃sje]
food products	**produits** (m pl) **alimentaires**	[prɔdyi alimɑ̃tɛr]
funeral home	**maison** (f) **funéraire**	[mɛzɔ̃ fynerɛr]
furniture (e.g., house ~)	**meubles** (m pl)	[mœbl]
garment	**vêtement** (m)	[vɛtmɑ̃]
hotel	**hôtel** (m)	[otɛl]
ice-cream	**glace** (f)	[glas]
industry	**industrie** (f)	[ɛ̃dystri]
insurance	**assurance** (f)	[asyrɑ̃s]
Internet	**Internet** (m)	[ɛ̃tɛrnɛt]
investment	**investissements** (m pl)	[ɛ̃vɛstismɑ̃]
jeweler	**bijoutier** (m)	[biʒutje]
jewelry	**bijouterie** (f)	[biʒutri]
laundry (shop)	**blanchisserie** (f)	[blɑ̃ʃisri]
legal advisor	**service** (m) **juridique**	[sɛrvis ʒyridik]
light industry	**industrie** (f) **légère**	[ɛ̃dystri leʒɛr]
magazine	**revue** (f)	[rəvy]
mail-order selling	**vente** (f) **par catalogue**	[vɑ̃t par katalɔg]
medicine	**médecine** (f)	[medsin]
movie theater	**cinéma** (m)	[sinema]
museum	**musée** (m)	[myze]
news agency	**agence** (f) **d'information**	[aʒɑ̃s dɛ̃fɔrmasjɔ̃]
newspaper	**journal** (m)	[ʒurnal]
nightclub	**boîte** (f) **de nuit**	[bwat də nɥi]

oil (petroleum)	pétrole (m)	[petrɔl]
parcels service	coursiers (m pl)	[kursje]
pharmaceuticals	industrie (f) pharmaceutique	[ɛ̃dystri farmasøtik]
printing (industry)	imprimerie (f)	[ɛ̃primri]
publishing house	maison (f) d'édition	[mɛzɔ̃ dedisjɔ̃]

radio (~ station)	radio (f)	[radjo]
real estate	immobilier (m)	[imɔbilje, -ɛr]
restaurant	restaurant (m)	[rɛstɔrɑ̃]

security agency	agence (f) de sécurité	[aʒɑ̃s də sekyrite]
sports	sport (m)	[spɔr]
stock exchange	bourse (f)	[burs]
store	magasin (m)	[magazɛ̃]
supermarket	supermarché (m)	[sypɛrmarʃe]
swimming pool	piscine (f)	[pisin]

tailors	atelier (m) de couture	[atəlje də kutyr]
television	télévision (f)	[televizjɔ̃]
theater	théâtre (m)	[teɑtr]
trade	commerce (m)	[kɔmɛrs]
transportation	sociétés de transport	[sɔsjete trɑ̃spɔr]
travel	tourisme (m)	[turism]

veterinarian	vétérinaire (m)	[veterinɛr]
warehouse	entrepôt (m)	[ɑ̃trəpo]
waste collection	récupération (f) des déchets	[rekyperasjɔ̃ də deʃɛ]

Job. Business. Part 2

83. Show. Exhibition

exhibition, show	salon (m)	[salɔ̃]
trade show	salon (m) commercial	[salɔ̃ kɔmɛrsjal]
participation	participation (f)	[partisipɑsjɔ̃]
to participate (vi)	participer à ...	[partisipe a]
participant (exhibitor)	participant (m)	[partisipɑ̃]
director	directeur (m)	[dirɛktœr]
organizer's office	direction (f)	[dirɛksjɔ̃]
organizer	organisateur (m)	[ɔrganizatœr]
to organize (vt)	organiser (vt)	[ɔrganize]
participation form	demande (f) de participation	[dəmɑ̃d də partisipɑsjɔ̃]
to fill out (vt)	remplir (vt)	[rɑ̃plir]
details	détails (m pl)	[detaj]
information	information (f)	[ɛ̃fɔrmasjɔ̃]
price	prix (m)	[pri]
including	y compris	[i kɔ̃pri]
to include (vt)	inclure (vt)	[ɛ̃klyr]
to pay (vi, vt)	payer (vi, vt)	[peje]
registration fee	droits (m pl) d'inscription	[drwa dɛ̃skripsjɔ̃]
entrance	entrée (f)	[ɑ̃tre]
pavilion, hall	pavillon (m)	[pavijɔ̃]
to register (vt)	enregistrer (vt)	[ɑ̃rəʒistre]
badge (identity tag)	badge (m)	[badʒ]
booth, stand	stand (m)	[stɑ̃d]
to reserve, to book	réserver (vt)	[rezɛrve]
display case	vitrine (f)	[vitrin]
spotlight	lampe (f)	[lɑ̃p]
design	design (m)	[dizajn]
to place (put, set)	mettre, placer	[mɛtr], [plase]
to be placed	être placé	[ɛtr plase]
distributor	distributeur (m)	[distribytœr]
supplier	fournisseur (m)	[furnisœr]
to supply (vt)	fournir (vt)	[furnir]
country	pays (m)	[pei]

| foreign (adj) | étranger (adj) | [etrɑ̃ʒe] |
| product | produit (m) | [prɔdyi] |

association	association (f)	[asɔsjasjɔ̃]
conference hall	salle (f) de conférences	[sal də kɔ̃ferɑ̃s]
congress	congrès (m)	[kɔ̃grɛ]
contest (competition)	concours (m)	[kɔ̃kur]

visitor	visiteur (m)	[vizitœr]
to visit (attend)	visiter (vt)	[vizite]
customer	client (m)	[klijɑ̃]

84. Science. Research. Scientists

science	science (f)	[sjɑ̃s]
scientific (adj)	scientifique (adj)	[sjɑ̃tifik]
scientist	savant (m)	[savɑ̃]
theory	théorie (f)	[teɔri]

axiom	axiome (m)	[aksjom]
analysis	analyse (f)	[analiz]
to analyze (vt)	analyser (vt)	[analize]
argument (strong ~)	argument (m)	[argymɑ̃]
substance (matter)	substance (f)	[sypstɑ̃s]

hypothesis	hypothèse (f)	[ipotɛz]
dilemma	dilemme (m)	[dilɛm]
dissertation	thèse (f)	[tɛz]
dogma	dogme (m)	[dɔgm]

doctrine	doctrine (f)	[dɔktrin]
research	recherche (f)	[rəʃɛrʃ]
to do research	rechercher (vt)	[rəʃɛrʃe]
testing	test (m)	[tɛst]
laboratory	laboratoire (m)	[labɔratwar]

method	méthode (f)	[metɔd]
molecule	molécule (f)	[mɔlekyl]
monitoring	monitoring (m)	[mɔnitɔriŋ]
discovery (act, event)	découverte (f)	[dekuvɛrt]

postulate	postulat (m)	[pɔstyla]
principle	principe (m)	[prɛ̃sip]
forecast	prévision (f)	[previzjɔ̃]
prognosticate (vt)	prévoir (vt)	[prevwar]

synthesis	synthèse (f)	[sɛ̃tɛz]
trend (tendency)	tendance (f)	[tɑ̃dɑ̃s]
theorem	théorème (m)	[teɔrɛm]
teachings	enseignements (m pl)	[ɑ̃sɛɲmɑ̃]

fact	**fait** (m)	[fɛ]
expedition	**expédition** (f)	[ɛkspedisjɔ̃]
experiment	**expérience** (f)	[ɛksperjɑ̃s]
academician	**académicien** (m)	[akademisjɛn]
bachelor (e.g., ~ of Arts)	**bachelier** (m)	[baʃəlje]
doctor (PhD)	**docteur** (m)	[dɔktœr]
Associate Professor	**chargé** (m) **de cours**	[ʃarʒe də kur]
Master (e.g., ~ of Arts)	**magistère** (m)	[maʒistɛr]
professor	**professeur** (m)	[prɔfɛsœr]

Professions and occupations

85. Job search. Dismissal

job	**travail** (m)	[travaj]
staff (work force)	**employés** (pl)	[ãplwaje]
personnel	**personnel** (m)	[pɛrsɔnɛl]
career	**carrière** (f)	[karjɛr]
prospects	**perspective** (f)	[pɛrspɛktiv]
skills (mastery)	**maîtrise** (f)	[metriz]
selection (screening)	**sélection** (f)	[selɛksjõ]
employment agency	**agence** (f)	[aʒãs
	de recrutement	də rəkrytmã]
résumé	**C.V.** (m)	[seve]
interview (for job)	**entretien** (m)	[ãtrətjɛ̃]
vacancy, opening	**emploi** (m) **vacant**	[ãplwa vakã]
salary, pay	**salaire** (m)	[salɛr]
fixed salary	**salaire** (m) **fixe**	[salɛr fiks]
pay, compensation	**rémunération** (f)	[remynerasjõ]
position (job)	**poste** (m)	[pɔst]
duty (of employee)	**fonction** (f)	[fõksjõ]
range of duties	**liste** (f) **des fonctions**	[list de fõksjõ]
busy (I'm ~)	**occupé** (adj)	[ɔkype]
to fire (dismiss)	**licencier** (vt)	[lisãsje]
dismissal	**licenciement** (m)	[lisãsimã]
unemployment	**chômage** (m)	[ʃomaʒ]
unemployed (n)	**chômeur** (m)	[ʃomœr]
retirement	**retraite** (f)	[rətrɛt]
to retire (from job)	**prendre sa retraite**	[prãdr sa rətrɛt]

86. Business people

director	**directeur** (m)	[dirɛktœr]
manager (director)	**gérant** (m)	[ʒerã]
boss	**patron** (m)	[patrõ]
superior	**supérieur** (m)	[syperjœr]
superiors	**supérieurs** (m pl)	[syperjœr]

| president | président (m) | [prezidɑ̃] |
| chairman | président (m) | [prezidɑ̃] |

deputy (substitute)	adjoint (m)	[adʒwɛ̃]
assistant	assistant (m)	[asistɑ̃]
secretary	secrétaire (m, f)	[səkretɛr]
personal assistant	secrétaire (m, f) personnel	[səkretɛr pɛrsɔnɛl]

businessman	homme (m) d'affaires	[ɔm dafɛr]
entrepreneur	entrepreneur (m)	[ɑ̃trəprənœr]
founder	fondateur (m)	[fɔ̃datœr]
to found (vt)	fonder (vt)	[fɔ̃de]

incorporator	fondateur (m)	[fɔ̃datœr]
partner	partenaire (m)	[partənɛr]
stockholder	actionnaire (m)	[aksjɔnɛr]

millionaire	millionnaire (m)	[miljɔnɛr]
billionaire	milliardaire (m)	[miljardɛr]
owner, proprietor	propriétaire (m)	[prɔprijetɛr]
landowner	propriétaire (m) foncier	[prɔprijetɛr fɔ̃sje]

| client | client (m) | [klijɑ̃] |
| regular client | client (m) régulier | [klijɑ̃ regylje] |

| buyer (customer) | acheteur (m) | [aʃtœr] |
| visitor | visiteur (m) | [vizitœr] |

professional (n)	professionnel (m)	[prɔfɛsjɔnɛl]
expert	expert (m)	[ɛkspɛr]
specialist	spécialiste (m)	[spesjalist]

| banker | banquier (m) | [bɑ̃kje] |
| broker | courtier (m) | [kurtje] |

cashier, teller	caissier (m)	[kesje]
accountant	comptable (m)	[kɔ̃tabl]
security guard	agent (m) de sécurité	[aʒɑ̃ də sekyrite]

| investor | investisseur (m) | [ɛ̃vɛstisœr] |
| debtor | débiteur (m) | [debitœr] |

| creditor | créancier (m) | [kreɑ̃sje] |
| borrower | emprunteur (m) | [ɑ̃prœ̃tœr] |

| importer | importateur (m) | [ɛ̃pɔrtatœr] |
| exporter | exportateur (m) | [ɛkspɔrtatœr] |

manufacturer	producteur (m)	[prɔdyktœr]
distributor	distributeur (m)	[distribytœr]
middleman	intermédiaire (m)	[ɛ̃tɛrmedjɛr]
consultant	conseiller (m)	[kɔ̃seje]

sales representative	représentant (m)	[rəprezãtã]
agent	agent (m)	[aʒã]
insurance agent	agent (m) d'assurances	[aʒã dasyrãs]

87. Service professions

cook	cuisinier (m)	[kɥizinje]
chef (kitchen chef)	cuisinier (m) en chef	[kɥizinje ã ʃɛf]
baker	boulanger (m)	[bulãʒe]

bartender	barman (m)	[barman]
waiter	serveur (m)	[sɛrvœr]
waitress	serveuse (f)	[sɛrvøz]

lawyer, attorney	avocat (m)	[avɔka]
lawyer (legal expert)	juriste (m)	[ʒyrist]
notary	notaire (m)	[nɔtɛr]

electrician	électricien (m)	[elɛktrisjɛ̃]
plumber	plombier (m)	[plõbje]
carpenter	charpentier (m)	[ʃarpãtje]

masseur	masseur (m)	[masœr]
masseuse	masseuse (f)	[masøz]
doctor	médecin (m)	[medsɛ̃]

taxi driver	chauffeur (m) de taxi	[ʃofœr də taksi]
driver	chauffeur (m)	[ʃofœr]
delivery man	livreur (m)	[livrœr]

chambermaid	femme (f) de chambre	[fam də ʃãbr]
security guard	agent (m) de sécurité	[aʒã də sekyrite]
flight attendant	hôtesse (f) de l'air	[otɛs də lɛr]

teacher (in primary school)	professeur (m)	[prɔfɛsœr]
librarian	bibliothécaire (m)	[biblijɔtekɛr]
translator	traducteur (m)	[tradyktœr]

interpreter	interprète (m)	[ɛ̃tɛrprɛt]
guide	guide (m)	[gid]

hairdresser	coiffeur (m)	[kwafœr]
mailman	facteur (m)	[faktœr]
salesman (store staff)	vendeur (m)	[vãdœr]

gardener	jardinier (m)	[ʒardinje]
domestic servant	serviteur (m)	[sɛrvitœr]

maid	servante (f)	[sɛrvãt]
cleaner (cleaning lady)	femme (f) de ménage	[fam də menaʒ]

88. Military professions and ranks

private	soldat (m)	[sɔlda]
sergeant	sergent (m)	[sɛrʒɑ̃]
lieutenant	lieutenant (m)	[ljøtnɑ̃]
captain	capitaine (m)	[kapitɛn]

major	commandant (m)	[kɔmɑ̃dɑ̃]
colonel	colonel (m)	[kɔlɔnɛl]
general	général (m)	[ʒeneral]
marshal	maréchal (m)	[mareʃal]
admiral	amiral (m)	[amiral]

military man	militaire (m)	[militɛr]
soldier	soldat (m)	[sɔlda]
officer	officier (m)	[ɔfisje]
commander	commandant (m)	[kɔmɑ̃dɑ̃]

border guard	garde-frontière (m)	[gardəfrɔ̃tjɛr]
radio operator	opérateur (m) radio	[ɔperatœr radjo]
scout (searcher)	éclaireur (m)	[eklɛrœr]
pioneer (sapper)	démineur (m)	[deminœr]
marksman	tireur (m)	[tirœr]
navigator	navigateur (m)	[navigatœr]

89. Officials. Priests

| king | roi (m) | [rwa] |
| queen | reine (f) | [rɛn] |

| prince | prince (m) | [prɛ̃s] |
| princess | princesse (f) | [prɛ̃sɛs] |

| tsar, czar | tsar (m) | [tsar] |
| czarina | tsarine (f) | [tsarin] |

president	président (m)	[prezidɑ̃]
Secretary (~ of State)	ministre (m)	[ministr]
prime minister	premier ministre (m)	[prəmje ministɛr]
senator	sénateur (m)	[senatœr]

diplomat	diplomate (m)	[diplɔmat]
consul	consul (m)	[kɔ̃syl]
ambassador	ambassadeur (m)	[ɑ̃basadœr]
advisor (military ~)	conseiller (m)	[kɔ̃seje]

official (civil servant)	fonctionnaire (m)	[fɔ̃ksjɔnɛr]
prefect	préfet (m)	[prefɛ]
mayor	maire (m)	[mɛr]

| judge | juge (m) | [ʒyʒ] |
| district attorney (prosecutor) | procureur (m) | [prɔkyrœr] |

missionary	missionnaire (m)	[misjɔnɛr]
monk	moine (m)	[mwan]
abbot	abbé (m)	[abe]
rabbi	rabbin (m)	[rabɛ̃]

vizier	vizir (m)	[vizir]
shah	shah (m)	[ʃa]
sheikh	cheik (m)	[ʃɛjk]

90. Agricultural professions

beekeeper	apiculteur (m)	[apikyltœr]
herder, shepherd	berger (m)	[bɛrʒe]
agronomist	agronome (m)	[agrɔnɔm]
cattle breeder	éleveur (m)	[elvœr]
veterinarian	vétérinaire (m)	[veterinɛr]

farmer	fermier (m)	[fɛrmje]
winemaker	vinificateur (m)	[vinifikatœr]
zoologist	zoologiste (m)	[zɔɔlɔʒist]
cowboy	cow-boy (m)	[kɔbɔj]

91. Art professions

| actor | acteur (m) | [aktœr] |
| actress | actrice (f) | [aktris] |

| singer (masc.) | chanteur (m) | [ʃɑ̃tœr] |
| singer (fem.) | cantatrice (f) | [kɑ̃tatris] |

| dancer (masc.) | danseur (m) | [dɑ̃sœr] |
| dancer (fem.) | danseuse (f) | [dɑ̃søz] |

| performing artist (masc.) | artiste (m) | [artist] |
| performing artist (fem.) | artiste (f) | [artist] |

musician	musicien (m)	[myzisjɛ̃]
pianist	pianiste (m)	[pjanist]
guitar player	guitariste (m)	[gitarist]

conductor (orchestra ~)	chef (m) d'orchestre	[ʃɛf dɔrkɛstr]
composer	compositeur (m)	[kɔ̃pozitœr]
impresario	imprésario (m)	[ɛ̃presarjo]
movie director	metteur (m) en scène	[mɛtœr ɑ̃ sɛn]

producer	producteur (m)	[prɔdyktœr]
scriptwriter	scénariste (m)	[senarist]
critic	critique (m)	[kritik]

writer	écrivain (m)	[ekrivɛ̃]
poet	poète (m)	[pɔɛt]
sculptor	sculpteur (m)	[skyltœr]
artist (painter)	peintre (m)	[pɛ̃tr]

juggler	jongleur (m)	[ʒɔ̃glœr]
clown	clown (m)	[klun]
acrobat	acrobate (m)	[akrɔbat]
magician	magicien (m)	[maʒisjɛ̃]

92. Various professions

doctor	médecin (m)	[medsɛ̃]
nurse	infirmière (f)	[ɛ̃firmjɛr]
psychiatrist	psychiatre (m)	[psikjatr]
dentist	stomatologue (m)	[stɔmatɔlɔg]
surgeon	chirurgien (m)	[ʃiryrʒjɛ̃]

astronaut	astronaute (m)	[astrɔnot]
astronomer	astronome (m)	[astrɔnɔm]
pilot	pilote (m)	[pilɔt]

driver (of taxi, etc.)	chauffeur (m)	[ʃofœr]
engineer (train driver)	conducteur (m) de train	[kɔ̃dyktœr də trɛ̃]
mechanic	mécanicien (m)	[mekanisjɛ̃]

miner	mineur (m)	[minœr]
worker	ouvrier (m)	[uvrije]
metalworker	serrurier (m)	[seryrje]
joiner (carpenter)	menuisier (m)	[mənɥizje]
turner	tourneur (m)	[turnœr]
construction worker	ouvrier (m) du bâtiment	[uvrije dy batimɑ̃]
welder	soudeur (m)	[sudœr]

professor (title)	professeur (m)	[prɔfɛsœr]
architect	architecte (m)	[arʃitɛkt]
historian	historien (m)	[istɔrjɛ̃]
scientist	savant (m)	[savɑ̃]
physicist	physicien (m)	[fizisjɛ̃]
chemist (scientist)	chimiste (m)	[ʃimist]

archeologist	archéologue (m)	[arkeɔlɔg]
geologist	géologue (m)	[ʒeɔlɔg]
researcher	chercheur (m)	[ʃɛrʃœr]
babysitter	baby-sitter (m, f)	[bebisitœr]
teacher, educator	pédagogue (m, f)	[pedagɔg]

editor	rédacteur (m)	[redaktœr]
editor-in-chief	rédacteur (m) en chef	[redaktœr ɑ̃ ʃɛf]
correspondent	correspondant (m)	[kɔrɛspɔ̃dɑ̃]
typist (fem.)	dactylographe (f)	[daktilɔgraf]

designer	designer (m)	[dizajnœr]
computer expert	informaticien (m)	[ɛ̃fɔrmatisjɛ̃]
programmer	programmeur (m)	[prɔgramœr]
engineer (designer)	ingénieur (m)	[ɛ̃ʒenjœr]

sailor	marin (m)	[marɛ̃]
seaman	matelot (m)	[matlo]
rescuer	secouriste (m)	[səkurist]

fireman	pompier (m)	[pɔ̃pje]
policeman	policier (m)	[pɔlisje]
watchman	veilleur (m) de nuit	[vejœr də nɥi]
detective	détective (m)	[detɛktiv]

customs officer	douanier (m)	[dwanje]
bodyguard	garde (m) du corps	[gard dy kɔr]
prison guard	gardien (m) de prison	[gardjɛ̃ də prizɔ̃]
inspector	inspecteur (m)	[ɛ̃spɛktœr]

sportsman	sportif (m)	[spɔrtif]
trainer, coach	entraîneur (m)	[ɑ̃trɛnœr]
butcher	boucher (m)	[buʃe]
cobbler	cordonnier (m)	[kɔrdɔnje]
merchant	commerçant (m)	[kɔmɛrsɑ̃]
loader (person)	chargeur (m)	[ʃarʒœr]

fashion designer	couturier (m)	[kutyrje]
model (fem.)	modèle (f)	[mɔdɛl]

93. Occupations. Social status

schoolboy	écolier (m)	[ekɔlje]
student (college ~)	étudiant (m)	[etydjɑ̃]

philosopher	philosophe (m)	[filɔzɔf]
economist	économiste (m)	[ekɔnɔmist]
inventor	inventeur (m)	[ɛ̃vɑ̃tœr]

unemployed (n)	chômeur (m)	[ʃomœr]
retiree	retraité (m)	[rətrɛte]
spy, secret agent	espion (m)	[ɛspjɔ̃]

prisoner	prisonnier (m)	[prizɔnje]
striker	gréviste (m)	[grevist]
bureaucrat	bureaucrate (m)	[byrokrat]

traveler	**voyageur** (m)	[vwajaʒœr]
homosexual	**homosexuel** (m)	[ɔmɔsɛksɥɛl]
hacker	**hacker** (m)	[akeːr]
hippie	**hippie** (m, f)	[ipi]
bandit	**bandit** (m)	[bɑ̃di]
hit man, killer	**tueur** (m) **à gages**	[tɥœr ɑ gaʒ]
drug addict	**drogué** (m)	[drɔge]
drug dealer	**trafiquant** (m) **de drogue**	[trafikɑ̃ də drɔg]
prostitute (fem.)	**prostituée** (f)	[prɔstitɥe]
pimp	**souteneur** (m)	[sutnœr]
sorcerer	**sorcier** (m)	[sɔrsje]
sorceress	**sorcière** (f)	[sɔrsjɛr]
pirate	**pirate** (m)	[pirat]
slave	**esclave** (m)	[ɛsklav]
samurai	**samouraï** (m)	[samuraj]
savage (primitive)	**sauvage** (m)	[sovaʒ]

Education

94. School

school	**école** (f)	[ekɔl]
headmaster	**directeur** (m) **d'école**	[dirɛktœr dekɔl]
pupil (boy)	**élève** (m)	[elɛv]
pupil (girl)	**élève** (f)	[elɛv]
schoolboy	**écolier** (m)	[ekɔlje]
schoolgirl	**écolière** (f)	[ekɔljɛr]
to teach (sb)	**enseigner** (vt)	[ɑ̃seɲe]
to learn (language, etc.)	**apprendre** (vt)	[aprɑ̃dr]
to learn by heart	**apprendre par cœur**	[aprɑ̃dr par kœr]
to study (work to learn)	**apprendre** (vi)	[aprɑ̃dr]
to be in school	**être étudiant, -e**	[ɛtr etydjɑ̃, -ɑ̃t]
to go to school	**aller à l'école**	[ale ɑ lekɔl]
alphabet	**alphabet** (m)	[alfabɛ]
subject (at school)	**matière** (f)	[matjɛr]
classroom	**salle** (f) **de classe**	[sal də klas]
lesson	**leçon** (f)	[ləsɔ̃]
recess	**récréation** (f)	[rekreasjɔ̃]
school bell	**sonnerie** (f)	[sɔnri]
school desk	**pupitre** (m)	[pypitr]
chalkboard	**tableau** (m)	[tablo]
grade	**note** (f)	[nɔt]
good grade	**bonne note** (f)	[bɔnnɔt]
bad grade	**mauvaise note** (f)	[movɛz nɔt]
to give a grade	**donner une note**	[dɔne yn nɔt]
mistake, error	**faute** (f)	[fot]
to make mistakes	**faire des fautes**	[fɛr de fot]
to correct (an error)	**corriger** (vt)	[kɔriʒe]
cheat sheet	**antisèche** (f)	[ɑ̃tisɛʃ]
homework	**devoir** (m)	[dəvwar]
exercise (in education)	**exercice** (m)	[ɛgzɛrsis]
to be present	**être présent**	[ɛtr prezɑ̃]
to be absent	**être absent**	[ɛtr apsɑ̃]
to miss school	**manquer l'école**	[mɑ̃ke lekɔl]

to punish (vt)	punir (vt)	[pynir]
punishment	punition (f)	[pynisjɔ̃]
conduct (behavior)	conduite (f)	[kɔ̃dɥit]

report card	carnet (m) de notes	[karnɛ də nɔt]
pencil	crayon (m)	[krɛjɔ̃]
eraser	gomme (f)	[gɔm]
chalk	craie (f)	[krɛ]
pencil case	plumier (m)	[plymje]

schoolbag	cartable (m)	[kartabl]
pen	stylo (m)	[stilo]
school notebook	cahier (m)	[kaje]
textbook	manuel (m)	[manɥɛl]
compasses	compas (m)	[kɔ̃pa]

to draw (a blueprint, etc.)	dessiner (vt)	[desine]
technical drawing	dessin (m) technique	[desɛ̃ tɛknik]

poem	poésie (f)	[pɔezi]
by heart (adv)	par cœur (adv)	[par kœr]
to learn by heart	apprendre par cœur	[aprɑ̃dr par kœr]

school vacation	vacances (f pl)	[vakɑ̃s]
to be on vacation	être en vacances	[ɛtr ɑ̃ vakɑ̃s]
to spend one's vacation	passer les vacances	[pɑse le vakɑ̃s]

test (written math ~)	interrogation (f) écrite	[ɛ̃terɔgasjɔ̃ ekrit]
essay (composition)	composition (f)	[kɔ̃pozisjɔ̃]
dictation	dictée (f)	[dikte]
exam	examen (m)	[ɛgzamɛ̃]
to take an exam	passer les examens	[pɑse lezɛgzamɛ̃]
experiment (chemical ~)	expérience (f)	[ɛksperjɑ̃s]

95. College. University

academy	académie (f)	[akademi]
university	université (f)	[ynivɛrsite]
faculty (section)	faculté (f)	[fakylte]

student (masc.)	étudiant (m)	[etydjɑ̃]
student (fem.)	étudiante (f)	[etydjɑ̃t]
lecturer (teacher)	enseignant (m)	[ɑ̃sɛɲɑ̃]

lecture hall, room	salle (f)	[sal]
graduate	licencié (m)	[lisɑ̃sje]
diploma	diplôme (m)	[diplom]
dissertation	thèse (f)	[tɛz]
study (report)	étude (f)	[etyd]
laboratory	laboratoire (m)	[labɔratwar]

lecture	cours (m)	[kur]
course mate	camarade (m) de cours	[kamarad də kur]
scholarship	bourse (f)	[burs]
academic degree	grade (m) universitaire	[grad yniversiter]

96. Sciences. Disciplines

mathematics	mathématiques (f pl)	[matematik]
algebra	algèbre (f)	[alʒɛbr]
geometry	géométrie (f)	[ʒeɔmetri]

astronomy	astronomie (f)	[astrɔnɔmi]
biology	biologie (f)	[bjɔlɔʒi]
geography	géographie (f)	[ʒeɔgrafi]
geology	géologie (f)	[ʒeɔlɔʒi]
history	histoire (f)	[istwar]

medicine	médecine (f)	[medsin]
pedagogy	pédagogie (f)	[pedagɔʒi]
law	droit (m)	[drwa]

physics	physique (f)	[fizik]
chemistry	chimie (f)	[ʃimi]
philosophy	philosophie (f)	[filɔzɔfi]
psychology	psychologie (f)	[psikɔlɔʒi]

97. Writing system. Orthography

grammar	grammaire (f)	[gramɛr]
vocabulary	vocabulaire (m)	[vɔkabylɛr]
phonetics	phonétique (f)	[fɔnetik]

noun	nom (m)	[nɔ̃]
adjective	adjectif (m)	[adʒɛktif]
verb	verbe (m)	[vɛrb]
adverb	adverbe (m)	[advɛrb]

pronoun	pronom (m)	[prɔnɔ̃]
interjection	interjection (f)	[ɛ̃tɛrʒɛksjɔ̃]
preposition	préposition (f)	[prepozisjɔ̃]

root	racine (f)	[rasin]
ending	terminaison (f)	[tɛrminɛzɔ̃]
prefix	préfixe (m)	[prefiks]
syllable	syllabe (f)	[silab]
suffix	suffixe (m)	[syfiks]
stress mark	accent (m) tonique	[aksɑ̃ tɔnik]
apostrophe	apostrophe (f)	[apɔstrɔf]

period, dot	point (m)	[pwɛ̃]
comma	virgule (f)	[virgyl]
semicolon	point (m) virgule	[pwɛ̃ virgyl]

| colon | deux-points (m) | [døpwɛ̃] |
| ellipsis | points (m pl) de suspension | [pwɛ̃ də syspɑ̃sjɔ̃] |

| question mark | point (m) d'interrogation | [pwɛ̃ dɛ̃terɔgasjɔ̃] |
| exclamation point | point (m) d'exclamation | [pwɛ̃ dɛksklamasjɔ̃] |

| quotation marks | guillemets (m pl) | [gijmɛ] |
| in quotation marks | entre guillemets | [ɑ̃tr gijmɛ] |

| parenthesis | parenthèses (f pl) | [parɑ̃tɛz] |
| in parenthesis | entre parenthèses | [ɑ̃tr parɑ̃tɛz] |

hyphen	trait (m) d'union	[trɛ dynjɔ̃]
dash	tiret (m)	[tire]
space (between words)	blanc (m)	[blɑ̃]

| letter | lettre (f) | [lɛtr] |
| capital letter | majuscule (f) | [maʒyskyl] |

| vowel (n) | voyelle (f) | [vwajɛl] |
| consonant (n) | consonne (f) | [kɔ̃sɔn] |

sentence	proposition (f)	[prɔpozisjɔ̃]
subject	sujet (m)	[syʒɛ]
predicate	prédicat (m)	[predika]

line	ligne (f)	[liɲ]
on a new line	à la ligne	[alaliɲ]
paragraph	paragraphe (m)	[paragraf]

word	mot (m)	[mo]
group of words	groupe (m) de mots	[grup də mo]
expression	expression (f)	[ɛkspresjɔ̃]

| synonym | synonyme (m) | [sinɔnim] |
| antonym | antonyme (m) | [ɑ̃tɔnim] |

rule	règle (f)	[rɛgl]
exception	exception (f)	[ɛksɛpsjɔ̃]
correct (adj)	correct (adj)	[kɔrɛkt]

conjugation	conjugaison (f)	[kɔ̃ʒygɛzɔ̃]
declension	déclinaison (f)	[deklinɛzɔ̃]
nominal case	cas (m)	[ka]
question	question (f)	[kɛstjɔ̃]
to underline (vt)	souligner (vt)	[suliɲe]
dotted line	pointillé (m)	[pwɛ̃tije]

98. Foreign languages

language	**langue** (f)	[lɑ̃g]
foreign language	**langue** (f) **étrangère**	[lɑ̃g etrɑ̃ʒɛr]
to study (vt)	**étudier** (vt)	[etydje]
to learn (language, etc.)	**apprendre** (vt)	[aprɑ̃dr]
to read (vi, vt)	**lire** (vi, vt)	[lir]
to speak (vi, vt)	**parler** (vi)	[parle]
to understand (vt)	**comprendre** (vt)	[kɔ̃prɑ̃dr]
to write (vt)	**écrire** (vt)	[ekrir]
fast (adv)	**vite** (adv)	[vit]
slowly (adv)	**lentement** (adv)	[lɑ̃tmɑ̃]
fluently (adv)	**couramment** (adv)	[kuramɑ̃]
rules	**règles** (f pl)	[rɛgl]
grammar	**grammaire** (f)	[gramɛr]
vocabulary	**vocabulaire** (m)	[vɔkabylɛr]
phonetics	**phonétique** (f)	[fɔnetik]
textbook	**manuel** (m)	[manɥɛl]
dictionary	**dictionnaire** (m)	[diksjɔnɛr]
teach-yourself book	**manuel** (m) **autodidacte**	[manɥɛl otodidakt]
phrasebook	**guide** (m) **de conversation**	[gid də kɔ̃vɛrsasjɔ̃]
cassette	**cassette** (f)	[kasɛt]
videotape	**cassette** (f) **vidéo**	[kasɛt video]
CD, compact disc	**CD** (m)	[sede]
DVD	**DVD** (m)	[devede]
alphabet	**alphabet** (m)	[alfabɛ]
to spell (vt)	**épeler** (vt)	[eple]
pronunciation	**prononciation** (f)	[prɔnɔ̃sjasjɔ̃]
accent	**accent** (m)	[aksɑ̃]
with an accent	**avec un accent**	[avɛk œn aksɑ̃]
without an accent	**sans accent**	[sɑ̃ zaksɑ̃]
word	**mot** (m)	[mo]
meaning	**sens** (m)	[sɑ̃s]
course (e.g., a French ~)	**cours** (m pl)	[kur]
to sign up	**s'inscrire** (vp)	[sɛ̃skrir]
teacher	**professeur** (m)	[prɔfɛsœr]
translation (process)	**traduction** (f)	[tradyksjɔ̃]
translation (text, etc.)	**traduction** (f)	[tradyksjɔ̃]
translator	**traducteur** (m)	[tradyktœr]
interpreter	**interprète** (m)	[ɛ̃tɛrprɛt]

| polyglot | polyglotte (m) | [poliglɔt] |
| memory | mémoire (f) | [memwar] |

Rest. Entertainment. Travel

99. Trip. Travel

tourism	tourisme (m)	[turism]
tourist	touriste (m)	[turist]
trip, voyage	voyage (m)	[vwajaʒ]
adventure	aventure (f)	[avɑ̃tyr]
trip, journey	voyage (m)	[vwajaʒ]
vacation	vacances (f pl)	[vakɑ̃s]
to be on vacation	être en vacances	[ɛtr ɑ̃ vakɑ̃s]
rest	repos (m)	[rəpo]
train	train (m)	[trɛ̃]
by train	en train	[ɑ̃ trɛ̃]
airplane	avion (m)	[avjɔ̃]
by airplane	en avion	[ɑn avjɔ̃]
by car	en voiture	[ɑ̃ vwatyr]
by ship	en bateau	[ɑ̃ bato]
luggage	bagage (m)	[bagaʒ]
suitcase, luggage	malle (f)	[mal]
luggage cart	chariot (m)	[ʃarjo]
passport	passeport (m)	[paspɔr]
visa	visa (m)	[viza]
ticket	ticket (m)	[tikɛ]
air ticket	billet (m) d'avion	[bijɛ davjɔ̃]
guidebook	guide (m)	[gid]
map	carte (f)	[kart]
area (rural ~)	région (f)	[reʒjɔ̃]
place, site	endroit (m)	[ɑ̃drwa]
exotic (n)	exotisme (m)	[ɛgzɔtism]
exotic (adj)	exotique (adj)	[ɛgzɔtik]
amazing (adj)	étonnant (adj)	[etɔnɑ̃]
group	groupe (m)	[grup]
excursion	excursion (f)	[ɛkskyrsjɔ̃]
guide (person)	guide (m)	[gid]

100. Hotel

hotel	hôtel (m)	[otɛl]
motel	motel (m)	[mɔtɛl]
three-star	3 étoiles	[trwa zetwal]
five-star	5 étoiles	[sɛ̆k etwal]
to stay (in hotel, etc.)	descendre (vi)	[desɑ̃dr]
room	chambre (f)	[ʃɑ̃br]
single room	chambre (f) simple	[ʃɑ̃br sɛ̆pl]
double room	chambre (f) double	[ʃɑ̃br dubl]
to book a room	réserver une chambre	[rezɛrve yn ʃɑ̃br]
half board	demi-pension (f)	[dəmipɑ̃sjɔ̃]
full board	pension (f) complète	[pɑ̃sjɔ̃ kɔ̃plɛt]
with bath	avec une salle de bain	[avɛk yn saldəbɛ̆]
with shower	avec une douche	[avɛk yn duʃ]
satellite television	télévision (f) par satellite	[televizjɔ̃ par satelit]
air-conditioner	climatiseur (m)	[klimatizœr]
towel	serviette (f)	[sɛrvjɛt]
key	clé, clef (f)	[kle]
administrator	administrateur (m)	[administratœr]
chambermaid	femme (f) de chambre	[fam də ʃɑ̃br]
porter, bellboy	porteur (m)	[pɔrtœr]
doorman	portier (m)	[pɔrtje]
restaurant	restaurant (m)	[rɛstɔrɑ̃]
pub, bar	bar (m)	[bar]
breakfast	petit déjeuner (m)	[pəti deʒœne]
dinner	dîner (m)	[dine]
buffet	buffet (m)	[byfɛ]
lobby	hall (m)	[ol]
elevator	ascenseur (m)	[asɑ̃sœr]
DO NOT DISTURB	PRIÈRE DE NE PAS DÉRANGER	[prijɛr dənəpɑ derɑ̃ʒe]
NO SMOKING	DÉFENSE DE FUMER	[defɑ̃s də fyme]

TECHNICAL EQUIPMENT. TRANSPORTATION

Technical equipment

101. Computer

computer	ordinateur (m)	[ɔrdinatœr]
notebook, laptop	PC (m) portable	[pese pɔrtabl]
to turn on	allumer (vt)	[alyme]
to turn off	éteindre (vt)	[etɛ̃dr]
keyboard	clavier (m)	[klavje]
key	touche (f)	[tuʃ]
mouse	souris (f)	[suri]
mouse pad	tapis (m) de souris	[tapi də suri]
button	bouton (m)	[butɔ̃]
cursor	curseur (m)	[kyrsœr]
monitor	moniteur (m)	[mɔnitœr]
screen	écran (m)	[ekrɑ̃]
hard disk	disque (m) dur	[disk dyr]
hard disk volume	capacité (f) du disque dur	[kapasite dy disk dyr]
memory	mémoire (f)	[memwar]
random access memory	mémoire (f) vive	[memwar viv]
file	fichier (m)	[fiʃje]
folder	dossier (m)	[dosje]
to open (vt)	ouvrir (vt)	[uvrir]
to close (vt)	fermer (vt)	[fɛrme]
to save (vt)	sauvegarder (vt)	[sovgarde]
to delete (vt)	supprimer (vt)	[syprime]
to copy (vt)	copier (vt)	[kɔpje]
to sort (vt)	trier (vt)	[trije]
to transfer (copy)	copier (vt)	[kɔpje]
program	programme (m)	[prɔgram]
software	logiciel (m)	[lɔʒisjɛl]
programmer	programmeur (m)	[prɔgramœr]
to program (vt)	programmer (vt)	[prɔgrame]
hacker	hacker (m)	[ake:r]
password	mot (m) de passe	[mo də pɑs]

virus	virus (m)	[virys]
to find, to detect	découvrir (vt)	[dekuvrir]
byte	bit (m)	[bit]
megabyte	mégabit (m)	[megabit]
data	données (f pl)	[dɔne]
database	base (f) de données	[baz də dɔne]
cable (USB, etc.)	câble (m)	[kabl]
to disconnect (vt)	déconnecter (vt)	[dekɔnɛkte]
to connect (sth to sth)	connecter (vt)	[kɔnɛkte]

102. Internet. E-mail

Internet	Internet (m)	[ɛ̃tɛrnɛt]
browser	navigateur (m)	[navigatœr]
search engine	moteur (m) de recherche	[mɔtœr də rəʃɛrʃ]
provider	fournisseur (m) d'accès	[furnisœr daksɛ]
web master	administrateur (m) de site	[administratœr də sit]
website	site (m) web	[sit wɛb]
web page	page (f) web	[paʒ wɛb]
address	adresse (f)	[adrɛs]
address book	carnet (m) d'adresses	[karnɛ dadrɛs]
mailbox	boîte (f) de réception	[bwat də resɛpsjɔ̃]
mail	courrier (m)	[kurje]
message	message (m)	[mesaʒ]
incoming messages	messages (pl) entrants	[mesaʒ ɑ̃trɑ̃]
outgoing messages	messages (pl) sortants	[mesaʒ sɔrtɑ̃]
sender	expéditeur (m)	[ɛkspeditœr]
to send (vt)	envoyer (vt)	[ɑ̃vwaje]
sending (of mail)	envoi (m)	[ɑ̃vwa]
receiver	destinataire (m)	[dɛstinatɛr]
to receive (vt)	recevoir (vt)	[rəsəvwar]
correspondence	correspondance (f)	[kɔrɛspɔ̃dɑ̃s]
to correspond (vi)	être en correspondance	[ɛtr ɑ̃ kɔrɛspɔ̃dɑ̃s]
file	fichier (m)	[fiʃje]
to download (vt)	télécharger (vt)	[teleʃarʒe]
to create (vt)	créer (vt)	[kree]
to delete (vt)	supprimer (vt)	[syprime]
deleted (adj)	supprimé (adj)	[syprime]
connection (ADSL, etc.)	connexion (f)	[kɔnɛksjɔ̃]

speed	vitesse (f)	[vitɛs]
modem	modem (m)	[mɔdɛm]
access	accès (m)	[aksɛ]
port (e.g., input ~)	port (m)	[pɔr]

| connection (make a ~) | connexion (f) | [kɔnɛksjõ] |
| to connect to ... (vi) | se connecter à ... | [sə kɔnɛkte a] |

| to select (vt) | sélectionner (vt) | [selɛksjɔne] |
| to search (for ...) | rechercher (vt) | [rəʃɛrʃe] |

103. Electricity

electricity	électricité (f)	[elɛktrisite]
electrical (adj)	électrique (adj)	[elɛktrik]
electric power station	centrale (f) électrique	[sãtral elɛktrik]
energy	énergie (f)	[enɛrʒi]
electric power	énergie (f) électrique	[enɛrʒi elɛktrik]

light bulb	ampoule (f)	[ãpul]
flashlight	torche (f)	[tɔrʃ]
street light	réverbère (m)	[revɛrbɛr]

light	lumière (f)	[lymjɛr]
to turn on	allumer (vt)	[alyme]
to turn off	éteindre (vt)	[etɛ̃dr]
to turn off the light	éteindre la lumière	[etɛ̃dr la lymjɛr]

to burn out (vi)	être grillé	[ɛtr grije]
short circuit	court-circuit (m)	[kursirkɥi]
broken wire	rupture (f)	[ryptyr]
contact	contact (m)	[kõtakt]

light switch	interrupteur (m)	[ɛ̃teryptœr]
wall socket	prise (f)	[priz]
plug	fiche (f)	[fiʃ]
extension cord	rallonge (f)	[ralõʒ]

fuse	fusible (m)	[fyzibl]
cable, wire	fil (m)	[fil]
wiring	installation (f) électrique	[ɛ̃stalasjõ elɛktrik]

ampere	ampère (m)	[ãpɛr]
amperage	intensité (f) du courant	[ɛ̃tãsite dy kurã]
volt	volt (m)	[vɔlt]
voltage	tension (f)	[tãsjõ]

electrical device	appareil (m) électrique	[aparɛj elɛktrik]
indicator	indicateur (m)	[ɛ̃dikatœr]
electrician	électricien (m)	[elɛktrisjɛ̃]

to solder (vt)	souder (vt)	[sude]
soldering iron	fer (m) à souder	[fɛr asude]
electric current	courant (m)	[kurɑ̃]

104. Tools

tool, instrument	outil (m)	[uti]
tools	outils (m pl)	[uti]
equipment (factory ~)	équipement (m)	[ekipmɑ̃]

hammer	marteau (m)	[marto]
screwdriver	tournevis (m)	[turnəvis]
ax	hache (f)	[aʃ]

saw	scie (f)	[si]
to saw (vt)	scier (vt)	[sje]
plane (tool)	rabot (m)	[rabo]
to plane (vt)	raboter (vt)	[rabote]
soldering iron	fer (m) à souder	[fɛr asude]
to solder (vt)	souder (vt)	[sude]
file (for metal)	lime (f)	[lim]
carpenter pincers	tenailles (f pl)	[tənɑj]
lineman's pliers	pince (f) plate	[pɛ̃s plat]
chisel	ciseau (m)	[sizo]

drill bit	foret (m)	[fɔrɛ]
electric drill	perceuse (f)	[pɛrsøz]
to drill (vi, vt)	percer (vt)	[pɛrse]

knife	couteau (m)	[kuto]
pocket knife	canif (m)	[kanif]
folding (~ knife)	pliant (adj)	[plijɑ̃]
blade	lame (f)	[lam]

sharp (blade, etc.)	bien affilé (adj)	[bjɛn afile]
blunt (adj)	émoussé (adj)	[emuse]
to become blunt	s'émousser (vp)	[semuse]
to sharpen (vt)	affiler (vt)	[afile]

bolt	boulon (m)	[bulɔ̃]
nut	écrou (m)	[ekru]
thread (of a screw)	filetage (m)	[filtaʒ]
wood screw	vis (f) à bois	[vi za bwa]

| nail | clou (m) | [klu] |
| nailhead | tête (f) de clou | [tɛt də klu] |

ruler (for measuring)	règle (f)	[rɛgl]
tape measure	mètre (m) à ruban	[mɛtr ɑ rybɑ̃]
spirit level	niveau (m) à bulle	[nivo ɑ byl]

magnifying glass	**loupe** (f)	[lup]
measuring instrument	**appareil** (m) **de mesure**	[aparɛj də məzyr]
to measure (vt)	**mesurer** (vt)	[məzyre]
scale (of thermometer, etc.)	**échelle** (f)	[eʃɛl]
readings	**relevé** (m)	[rəlve]
compressor	**compresseur** (m)	[kɔ̃presœr]
microscope	**microscope** (m)	[mikrɔskɔp]
pump (e.g., water ~)	**pompe** (f)	[pɔ̃p]
robot	**robot** (m)	[rɔbo]
laser	**laser** (m)	[lazɛr]
wrench	**clé** (f) **de serrage**	[kle də seraʒ]
adhesive tape	**ruban** (m) **adhésif**	[rybɑ̃ adezif]
glue	**colle** (f)	[kɔl]
emery paper	**papier** (m) **d'émeri**	[papje dɛmri]
spring	**ressort** (m)	[rəsɔr]
magnet	**aimant** (m)	[ɛmɑ̃]
gloves	**gants** (m pl)	[gɑ̃]
rope	**corde** (f)	[kɔrd]
cord	**cordon** (m)	[kɔrdɔ̃]
wire (e.g., telephone ~)	**fil** (m)	[fil]
cable	**câble** (m)	[kabl]
sledgehammer	**masse** (f)	[mas]
crowbar	**pic** (m)	[pik]
ladder	**escabeau** (m)	[ɛskabo]
stepladder	**échelle** (f) **double**	[eʃɛl dubl]
to screw (tighten)	**visser** (vt)	[vise]
to unscrew, untwist (vt)	**dévisser** (vt)	[devise]
to tighten (vt)	**serrer** (vt)	[sere]
to glue, to stick	**coller** (vt)	[kɔle]
to cut (vt)	**couper** (vt)	[kupe]
malfunction (fault)	**défaut** (m)	[defo]
repair (mending)	**réparation** (f)	[reparasjɔ̃]
to repair, to mend (vt)	**réparer** (vt)	[repare]
to adjust (machine, etc.)	**régler** (vt)	[regle]
to check (to examine)	**vérifier** (vt)	[verifje]
checking	**vérification** (f)	[verifikasjɔ̃]
readings	**relevé** (m)	[rəlve]
reliable (machine)	**fiable** (adj)	[fjabl]
complicated (adj)	**complexe** (adj)	[kɔ̃plɛks]
to rust (get rusted)	**rouiller** (vi)	[ruje]
rusty, rusted (adj)	**rouillé** (adj)	[ruje]
rust	**rouille** (f)	[ruj]

Transportation

105. Airplane

airplane	avion (m)	[avjɔ̃]
air ticket	billet (m) d'avion	[bijɛ davjɔ̃]
airline	compagnie (f) aérienne	[kɔ̃paɲi aerjɛn]
airport	aéroport (m)	[aeropɔr]
supersonic (adj)	supersonique (adj)	[sypɛrsɔnik]
captain	commandant (m) de bord	[kɔmãdã də bɔr]
crew	équipage (m)	[ekipaʒ]
pilot	pilote (m)	[pilɔt]
flight attendant	hôtesse (f) de l'air	[otɛs də lɛr]
navigator	navigateur (m)	[navigatœr]
wings	ailes (f pl)	[ɛl]
tail	queue (f)	[kø]
cockpit	cabine (f)	[kabin]
engine	moteur (m)	[mɔtœr]
undercarriage	train (m) d'atterrissage	[trɛ̃ daterisaʒ]
turbine	turbine (f)	[tyrbin]
propeller	hélice (f)	[elis]
black box	boîte (f) noire	[bwat nwar]
control column	gouvernail (m)	[guvɛrnaj]
fuel	carburant (m)	[karbyrã]
safety card	consigne (f) de sécurité	[kɔ̃siɲ də sekyrite]
oxygen mask	masque (m) à oxygène	[mask a ɔksiʒɛn]
uniform	uniforme (m)	[ynifɔrm]
life vest	gilet (m) de sauvetage	[ʒilɛ də sovtaʒ]
parachute	parachute (m)	[paraʃyt]
takeoff	décollage (m)	[dekɔlaʒ]
to take off (vi)	décoller (vi)	[dekɔle]
runway	piste (f) de décollage	[pist dekɔlaʒ]
visibility	visibilité (f)	[vizibilite]
flight (act of flying)	vol (m)	[vɔl]
altitude	altitude (f)	[altityd]
air pocket	trou (m) d'air	[tru dɛr]
seat	place (f)	[plas]
headphones	écouteurs (m pl)	[ekutœr]
folding tray	tablette (f)	[tablɛt]

airplane window	**hublot** (m)	[yblo]
aisle	**couloir** (m)	[kulwar]

106. Train

train	**train** (m)	[trɛ̃]
suburban train	**train** (m) **de banlieue**	[trɛ̃ də bɑ̃ljø]
express train	**TGV** (m)	[teʒeve]
diesel locomotive	**locomotive** (f) **diesel**	[lɔkɔmɔtiv djezɛl]
steam engine	**locomotive** (f) **à vapeur**	[lɔkɔmɔtiv ɑ vapœr]
passenger car	**wagon** (m)	[vagɔ̃]
dining car	**wagon-restaurant** (m)	[vagɔ̃rɛstɔrɑ̃]
rails	**rails** (m pl)	[raj]
railroad	**chemin** (m) **de fer**	[ʃəmɛ̃ də fɛr]
railway tie	**traverse** (f)	[travɛrs]
platform (railway ~)	**quai** (m)	[kɛ]
track (~ 1, 2, etc.)	**voie** (f)	[vwa]
semaphore	**sémaphore** (m)	[semafɔr]
station	**station** (f)	[stasjɔ̃]
engineer	**conducteur** (m) **de train**	[kɔ̃dyktœr də trɛ̃]
porter (of luggage)	**porteur** (m)	[pɔrtœr]
train steward	**steward** (m)	[stiwart]
passenger	**passager** (m)	[pɑsaʒe]
conductor	**contrôleur** (m)	[kɔ̃trolœr]
corridor (in train)	**couloir** (m)	[kulwar]
emergency break	**frein** (m) **d'urgence**	[frɛ̃ dyrʒɑ̃s]
compartment	**compartiment** (m)	[kɔ̃partimɑ̃]
berth	**couchette** (f)	[kuʃɛt]
upper berth	**couchette** (f) **d'en haut**	[kuʃɛt dɛ̃ o]
lower berth	**couchette** (f) **d'en bas**	[kuʃɛt dɛ̃ba]
bed linen	**linge** (m) **de lit**	[lɛ̃ʒ də li]
ticket	**ticket** (m)	[tikɛ]
schedule	**horaire** (m)	[ɔrɛr]
information display	**tableau** (m) **d'informations**	[tablo dɛ̃fɔrmasjɔ̃]
to leave, to depart	**partir** (vi)	[partir]
departure (of train)	**départ** (m)	[depar]
to arrive (ab. train)	**arriver** (vi)	[arive]
arrival	**arrivée** (f)	[arive]
to arrive by train	**arriver en train**	[arive ɑ̃ trɛ̃]
to get on the train	**prendre le train**	[prɑ̃dr lə trɛ̃]

to get off the train	descendre du train	[desɑ̃dr dy trɛ̃]
train wreck	accident (m) ferroviaire	[aksidɑ̃ ferɔvjɛr]
to be derailed	dérailler (vi)	[deraje]

steam engine	locomotive (f) à vapeur	[lɔkɔmɔtiv ɑ vapœr]
stoker, fireman	chauffeur (m)	[ʃofœr]
firebox	chauffe (f)	[ʃof]
coal	charbon (m)	[ʃarbɔ̃]

107. Ship

| ship | bateau (m) | [bato] |
| vessel | navire (m) | [navir] |

steamship	bateau (m) à vapeur	[bato ɑ vapœr]
riverboat	paquebot (m)	[pakbo]
ocean liner	bateau (m) de croisière	[bato də krwazjɛr]
cruiser	croiseur (m)	[krwazœr]

yacht	yacht (m)	[jot]
tugboat	remorqueur (m)	[rəmɔrkœr]
barge	péniche (f)	[peniʃ]
ferry	ferry (m)	[feri]

sailing ship	voilier (m)	[vwalje]
brigantine	brigantin (m)	[brigɑ̃tɛ̃]
ice breaker	brise-glace (m)	[brizglas]
submarine	sous-marin (m)	[sumarɛ̃]

boat (flat-bottomed ~)	canot (m) à rames	[kano ɑ ram]
dinghy	dinghy (m)	[diŋgi]
lifeboat	canot (m) de sauvetage	[kano də sovtaʒ]
motorboat	canot (m) à moteur	[kano ɑ mɔtœr]

captain	capitaine (m)	[kapitɛn]
seaman	matelot (m)	[matlo]
sailor	marin (m)	[marɛ̃]
crew	équipage (m)	[ekipaʒ]

boatswain	maître (m) d'équipage	[mɛtr dekipaʒ]
ship's boy	mousse (m)	[mus]
cook	cuisinier (m) du bord	[kɥizinje dy bɔr]
ship's doctor	médecin (m) de bord	[medsɛ̃ də bɔr]

deck	pont (m)	[pɔ̃]
mast	mât (m)	[mɑ]
sail	voile (f)	[vwal]
hold	cale (f)	[kal]
bow (prow)	proue (f)	[pru]
stern	poupe (f)	[pup]

| oar | rame (f) | [ram] |
| screw propeller | hélice (f) | [elis] |

cabin	cabine (f)	[kabin]
wardroom	carré (m) des officiers	[kare dezɔfisje]
engine room	salle (f) des machines	[sal de maʃin]
bridge	passerelle (f)	[pɑsrɛl]
radio room	cabine (f) de T.S.F.	[kabin də tesɛf]
wave (radio)	onde (f)	[ɔ̃d]
logbook	journal (m) de bord	[ʒurnal də bɔr]

spyglass	longue-vue (f)	[lɔ̃gvy]
bell	cloche (f)	[klɔʃ]
flag	pavillon (m)	[pavijɔ̃]
rope (mooring ~)	grosse corde (f) tressée	[gros kɔrd trese]
knot (bowline, etc.)	nœud (m) marin	[nø marɛ̃]

| deckrail | rampe (f) | [rɑ̃p] |
| gangway | passerelle (f) | [pɑsrɛl] |

anchor	ancre (f)	[ɑ̃kr]
to weigh anchor	lever l'ancre	[ləve lɑ̃kr]
to drop anchor	jeter l'ancre	[ʒəte lɑ̃kr]
anchor chain	chaîne (f) d'ancrage	[ʃɛn dɑ̃kraʒ]

port (harbor)	port (m)	[pɔr]
berth, wharf	embarcadère (m)	[ɑ̃barkadɛr]
to berth (moor)	accoster (vi)	[akɔste]
to cast off	larguer les amarres	[large lezamar]

trip, voyage	voyage (m)	[vwajaʒ]
cruise (sea trip)	croisière (f)	[krwazjɛr]
course (route)	cap (m)	[kap]
route (itinerary)	itinéraire (m)	[itinerɛr]

fairway	chenal (m)	[ʃənal]
shallows (shoal)	bas-fond (m)	[bafɔ̃]
to run aground	échouer sur un bas-fond	[eʃwe syr œ̃ bafɔ̃]

storm	tempête (f)	[tɑ̃pɛt]
signal	signal (m)	[siɲal]
to sink (vi)	sombrer (vi)	[sɔ̃bre]
Man overboard!	Un homme à la mer!	[ynɔm alamɛr]
SOS	SOS (m)	[ɛsoɛs]
ring buoy	bouée (f) de sauvetage	[bwe də sovtaʒ]

108. Airport

| airport | aéroport (m) | [aeropɔr] |
| airplane | avion (m) | [avjɔ̃] |

airline	compagnie (f) aérienne	[kɔ̃paɲi aerjɛn]
air-traffic controller	contrôleur (m) aérien	[kɔ̃trolœr aerjɛ̃]
departure	départ (m)	[depar]
arrival	arrivée (f)	[arive]
to arrive (by plane)	arriver (vi)	[arive]
departure time	temps (m) de départ	[tɑ̃ də depar]
arrival time	temps (m) d'arrivée	[tɑ̃ darive]
to be delayed	être retardé	[ɛtr rətarde]
flight delay	retard (m) de l'avion	[rətar də lavjɔ̃]
information board	tableau (m) d'informations	[tablo dɛformasjɔ̃]
information	information (f)	[ɛ̃formasjɔ̃]
to announce (vt)	annoncer (vt)	[anɔ̃se]
flight (e.g., next ~)	vol (m)	[vɔl]
customs	douane (f)	[dwan]
customs officer	douanier (m)	[dwanje]
customs declaration	déclaration (f) de douane	[deklarasjɔ̃ də dwan]
to fill out (vt)	remplir (vt)	[rɑ̃plir]
to fill out the declaration	remplir la déclaration	[rɑ̃plir la deklarasjɔ̃]
passport control	contrôle (m) de passeport	[kɔ̃trol də paspɔr]
luggage	bagage (m)	[bagaʒ]
hand luggage	bagage (m) à main	[bagaʒ a mɛ̃]
Lost Luggage Desk	service des objets trouvés	[sɛrvis de ɔbʒɛ truve]
luggage cart	chariot (m)	[ʃarjo]
landing	atterrissage (m)	[aterisaʒ]
landing strip	piste (f) d'atterrissage	[pist daterisaʒ]
to land (vi)	atterrir (vi)	[aterir]
airstairs	escalier (m) d'avion	[ɛskalje davjɔ̃]
check-in	enregistrement (m)	[ɑ̃rəʒistrəmɑ̃]
check-in desk	comptoir (m) d'enregistrement	[kɔ̃twar dɑ̃rəʒistrəmɑ̃]
to check-in (vi)	s'enregistrer (vp)	[sɑ̃rəʒistre]
boarding pass	carte (f) d'embarquement	[kart dɑ̃barkəmɑ̃]
departure gate	porte (f) d'embarquement	[pɔrt dɑ̃barkəmɑ̃]
transit	transit (m)	[trɑ̃zit]
to wait (vt)	attendre (vt)	[atɑ̃dr]
departure lounge	salle (f) d'attente	[sal datɑ̃t]
to see off	raccompagner (vt)	[rakɔ̃paɲe]
to say goodbye	dire au revoir	[dir ərəvwar]

Life events

109. Holidays. Event

celebration, holiday	fête (f)	[fɛt]
national day	fête (f) nationale	[fɛt nasjɔnal]
public holiday	jour (m) férié	[ʒur ferje]
to commemorate (vt)	célébrer (vt)	[selebre]
event (happening)	événement (m)	[evɛnmɑ̃]
event (organized activity)	événement (m)	[evɛnmɑ̃]
banquet (party)	banquet (m)	[bɑ̃kɛ]
reception (formal party)	réception (f)	[resɛpsjɔ̃]
feast	festin (m)	[fɛstɛ̃]
anniversary	anniversaire (m)	[anivɛrsɛr]
jubilee	jubilé (m)	[ʒybile]
to celebrate (vt)	fêter, célébrer	[fete], [selebre]
New Year	Nouvel An (m)	[nuvɛl ɑ̃]
Happy New Year!	Bonne année!	[bɔn ane]
Santa Claus	Père Noël (m)	[pɛr nɔɛl]
Christmas	Noël (m)	[nɔɛl]
Merry Christmas!	Joyeux Noël!	[ʒwajø nɔɛl]
Christmas tree	arbre (m) de Noël	[arbr də nɔɛl]
fireworks	feux (m pl) d'artifice	[fø dartifis]
wedding	mariage (m)	[marjaʒ]
groom	fiancé (m)	[fijɑ̃se]
bride	fiancée (f)	[fijɑ̃se]
to invite (vt)	inviter (vt)	[ɛ̃vite]
invitation card	lettre (f) d'invitation	[lɛtr dɛ̃vitasjɔ̃]
guest	invité (m)	[ɛ̃vite]
to visit (vt)	visiter (vt)	[vizite]
(~ your parents, etc.)		
to greet the guests	accueillir les invités	[akœjir lezɛ̃vite]
gift, present	cadeau (m)	[kado]
to give (sth as present)	offrir (vt)	[ɔfrir]
to receive gifts	recevoir des cadeaux	[rəsəvwar de kado]
bouquet (of flowers)	bouquet (m)	[bukɛ]
congratulations	félicitations (f pl)	[felisitasjɔ̃]
to congratulate (vt)	féliciter (vt)	[felisite]

greeting card	carte (f) de veux	[kart də vœ]
to send a postcard	envoyer une carte	[ãvwaje yn kart]
to get a postcard	recevoir une carte	[rəsəvwar yn kart]

toast	toast (m)	[tost]
to offer (a drink, etc.)	offrir (vt)	[ɔfrir]
champagne	champagne (m)	[ʃãpaɲ]

to have fun	s'amuser (vp)	[samyze]
fun, merriment	gaieté (f)	[gete]
joy (emotion)	joie (f)	[ʒwa]

| dance | danse (f) | [dãs] |
| to dance (vi, vt) | danser (vi, vt) | [dãse] |

| waltz | valse (f) | [vals] |
| tango | tango (m) | [tãgo] |

110. Funerals. Burial

cemetery	cimetière (m)	[simãtje]
grave, tomb	tombe (f)	[tõb]
cross	croix (f)	[krwa]
gravestone	pierre (f) tombale	[pjɛr tõbal]
fence	clôture (f)	[klotyr]
chapel	chapelle (f)	[ʃapɛl]

| death | mort (f) | [mɔr] |
| to die (vi) | mourir (vi) | [murir] |

| the deceased | défunt (m) | [defœ̃] |
| mourning | deuil (m) | [dœj] |

to bury (vt)	enterrer (vt)	[ãtere]
funeral home	maison (f) funéraire	[mɛzõ fynerɛr]
funeral	enterrement (m)	[ãtɛrmã]

| wreath | couronne (f) | [kurɔn] |
| casket | cercueil (m) | [sɛrkœj] |

| hearse | corbillard (m) | [kɔrbijar] |
| shroud | linceul (m) | [lɛ̃sœl] |

funeral procession	cortège (m) funèbre	[kɔrtɛʒ fynɛbr]
cremation urn	urne (f) funéraire	[yrn fynerɛr]
crematory	crématoire (m)	[krematwar]

obituary	nécrologue (m)	[nekrɔlɔg]
to cry (weep)	pleurer (vi)	[plœre]
to sob (vi)	sangloter (vi)	[sãglɔte]

111. War. Soldiers

platoon	section (f)	[sɛksjɔ̃]
company	compagnie (f)	[kɔ̃paɲi]
regiment	régiment (m)	[reʒimɑ̃]
army	armée (f)	[arme]
division	division (f)	[divizjɔ̃]

section, squad	détachement (m)	[detaʃmɑ̃]
host (army)	armée (f)	[arme]

soldier	soldat (m)	[sɔlda]
officer	officier (m)	[ɔfisje]

private	soldat (m)	[sɔlda]
sergeant	sergent (m)	[sɛrʒɑ̃]
lieutenant	lieutenant (m)	[ljøtnɑ̃]
captain	capitaine (m)	[kapitɛn]
major	commandant (m)	[kɔmɑ̃dɑ̃]
colonel	colonel (m)	[kɔlonɛl]
general	général (m)	[ʒeneral]

sailor	marin (m)	[marɛ̃]
captain	capitaine (m)	[kapitɛn]
boatswain	maître (m) d'équipage	[mɛtr dekipaʒ]

artilleryman	artilleur (m)	[artijœr]
paratrooper	parachutiste (m)	[paraʃytist]
pilot	pilote (m)	[pilɔt]
navigator	navigateur (m)	[navigatœr]
mechanic	mécanicien (m)	[mekanisjɛ̃]

pioneer (sapper)	démineur (m)	[deminœr]
parachutist	parachutiste (m)	[paraʃytist]
reconnaissance scout	éclaireur (m)	[eklɛrœr]
sniper	tireur (m) d'élite	[tirœr delit]

patrol (group)	patrouille (f)	[patruj]
to patrol (vt)	patrouiller (vi)	[patruje]
sentry, guard	sentinelle (f)	[sɑ̃tinɛl]

warrior	guerrier (m)	[gɛrje]
hero	héros (m)	[ero]
heroine	héroïne (f)	[erɔin]
patriot	patriote (m)	[patrijɔt]

traitor	traître (m)	[trɛtr]
to betray (vt)	trahir (vt)	[trair]

deserter	déserteur (m)	[dezɛrtœr]
to desert (vi)	déserter (vt)	[dezɛrte]

mercenary	mercenaire (m)	[mɛrsənɛr]
recruit	recrue (f)	[rəkry]
volunteer	volontaire (m)	[vɔlɔ̃tɛr]

dead (n)	mort (m)	[mɔr]
wounded (n)	blessé (m)	[blese]
prisoner of war	prisonnier (m) de guerre	[prizɔnje də gɛr]

112. War. Military actions. Part 1

war	guerre (f)	[gɛr]
to be at war	faire la guerre	[fɛr la gɛr]
civil war	guerre (f) civile	[gɛr sivil]

treacherously (adv)	perfidement (adv)	[pɛrfidmɑ̃]
declaration of war	déclaration (f) de guerre	[deklarasjɔ̃ də gɛr]
to declare (~ war)	déclarer (vt)	[deklare]
aggression	agression (f)	[agrɛsjɔ̃]
to attack (invade)	attaquer (vt)	[atake]

to invade (vt)	envahir (vt)	[ɑ̃vair]
invader	envahisseur (m)	[ɑ̃vaisœr]
conqueror	conquérant (m)	[kɔ̃kerɑ̃]

defense	défense (f)	[defɑ̃s]
to defend (a country, etc.)	défendre (vt)	[defɑ̃dr]
to defend oneself	se défendre (vp)	[sə defɑ̃dr]

enemy	ennemi (m)	[ɛnmi]
foe, adversary	adversaire (m)	[advɛrsɛr]
enemy (as adj)	ennemi (adj)	[ɛnmi]

| strategy | stratégie (f) | [strateʒi] |
| tactics | tactique (f) | [taktik] |

order	ordre (m)	[ɔrdr]
command (order)	commande (f)	[kɔmɑ̃d]
to order (vt)	ordonner (vt)	[ɔrdɔne]
mission	mission (f)	[misjɔ̃]
secret (adj)	secret (adj)	[səkrɛ]

| battle | bataille (f) | [bataj] |
| combat | combat (m) | [kɔ̃ba] |

attack	attaque (f)	[atak]
storming (assault)	assaut (m)	[aso]
to storm (vt)	prendre d'assaut	[prɑ̃dr daso]
siege (to be under ~)	siège (m)	[sjɛʒ]
offensive (n)	offensive (f)	[ɔfɑ̃siv]
to go on the offensive	passer à l'offensive	[pɑse a lɔfɑ̃siv]

| retreat | retraite (f) | [rətrɛt] |
| to retreat (vi) | faire retraite | [fɛr rətrɛt] |

| encirclement | encerclement (m) | [ãsɛrkləmã] |
| to encircle (vt) | encercler (vt) | [ãsɛrkle] |

bombing (by aircraft)	bombardement (m)	[bõbardəmã]
to drop a bomb	lancer une bombe	[lãse yn bõb]
to bomb (vt)	bombarder (vt)	[bõbarde]
explosion	explosion (f)	[ɛksplozjõ]

shot	coup (m) de feu	[ku də fø]
to fire a shot	tirer un coup de feu	[tire œ̃ ku də fø]
firing (burst of ~)	fusillade (f)	[fyzijad]

to take aim (at ...)	viser (vt)	[vize]
to point (a gun)	pointer (sur ...)	[pwɛ̃te syr]
to hit (the target)	atteindre (vt)	[atɛ̃dr]

to sink (~ a ship)	faire sombrer	[fɛr sõbre]
hole (in a ship)	trou (m)	[tru]
to founder, to sink (vi)	sombrer (vi)	[sõbre]

front (war ~)	front (m)	[frõ]
rear (homefront)	arrière front (m)	[arjɛr frõ]
evacuation	évacuation (f)	[evakɥasjõ]
to evacuate (vt)	évacuer (vt)	[evakɥe]

trench	tranchée (f)	[trãʃe]
barbwire	barbelés (m pl)	[barbəle]
barrier (anti tank ~)	barrage (m)	[baraʒ]
watchtower	tour (f) de guet	[tur də gɛ]

hospital	hôpital (m)	[ɔpital]
to wound (vt)	blesser (vt)	[blese]
wound	blessure (f)	[blesyr]
wounded (n)	blessé (m)	[blese]
to be wounded	être blessé	[ɛtr blese]
serious (wound)	grave (adj)	[grav]

113. War. Military actions. Part 2

captivity	captivité (f)	[kaptivite]
to take captive	captiver (vt)	[kaptive]
to be in captivity	être prisonnier	[ɛtr prizɔnje]
to be taken prisoner	être fait prisonnier	[ɛtr fɛ prizɔnje]

| concentration camp | camp (m) de concentration | [kã də kõsãtrasjõ] |
| prisoner of war | prisonnier (m) de guerre | [prizɔnje də gɛr] |

to escape (vi)	s'enfuir (vp)	[sɑ̃fчir]
to betray (vt)	trahir (vt)	[trair]
betrayer	traître (m)	[trɛtr]
betrayal	trahison (f)	[traizɔ̃]

to execute (shoot)	fusiller (vt)	[fyzije]
execution (by firing squad)	fusillade (f)	[fyzijad]

equipment (military gear)	équipement (m)	[ekipmɑ̃]
shoulder board	épaulette (f)	[epolɛt]
gas mask	masque (m) à gaz	[mask ɑ gaz]

radio transmitter	émetteur (m) radio	[emetœr radjo]
cipher, code	chiffre (m)	[ʃifr]
secrecy	conspiration (f)	[kɔ̃spirasjɔ̃]
password	mot (m) de passe	[mo də pɑs]

land mine	mine (f) terrestre	[min tɛrɛstr]
to mine (road, etc.)	miner (vt)	[mine]
minefield	champ (m) de mines	[ʃɑ̃ də min]

air-raid warning	alerte (f) aérienne	[alɛrt aerjɛ̃]
alarm (warning)	signal (m) d'alarme	[siɲal dalarm]
signal	signal (m)	[siɲal]
signal flare	fusée signal (f)	[fyze siɲal]

headquarters	état-major (m)	[eta maʒɔr]
reconnaissance	reconnaissance (f)	[rəkɔnɛsɑ̃s]
situation	situation (f)	[sitчasjɔ̃]
report	rapport (m)	[rapɔr]
ambush	embuscade (f)	[ɑ̃byskad]
reinforcement (of army)	renfort (m)	[rɑ̃fɔr]

target	cible (f)	[sibl]
proving ground	polygone (m)	[pɔligɔn]
military exercise	manœuvres (f pl)	[manœvr]

panic	panique (f)	[panik]
devastation	dévastation (f)	[devastasjɔ̃]
destruction, ruins	destructions (f pl)	[dɛstryksjɔ̃]
to destroy (vt)	détruire (vt)	[detrчir]

to survive (vi, vt)	survivre (vi)	[syrvivr]
to disarm (vt)	désarmer (vt)	[dezarme]
to handle (~ a gun)	manier (vt)	[manje]

Attention!	Garde-à-vous! Fixe!	[gardavu], [fiks]
At ease!	Repos!	[rəpo]

feat (of courage)	exploit (m)	[ɛksplwa]
oath (vow)	serment (m)	[sɛrmɑ̃]
to swear (an oath)	jurer (vi)	[ʒyre]

decoration (medal, etc.)	décoration (f)	[dekɔrasjɔ̃]
to award (give medal to)	décorer (vt)	[dekɔre]
medal	médaille (f)	[medaj]
order (e.g., ~ of Merit)	ordre (m)	[ɔrdr]

victory	victoire (f)	[viktwar]
defeat	défaite (f)	[defɛt]
armistice	armistice (m)	[armistis]

banner (standard)	drapeau (m)	[drapo]
glory (honor, fame)	gloire (f)	[glwar]
parade	défilé (m)	[defile]
to march (on parade)	marcher (vi)	[marʃe]

114. Weapons

weapons	arme (f)	[arm]
firearm	armes (f pl) à feu	[arm ɑ fø]
cold weapons (knives, etc.)	armes (f pl) blanches	[arm blɑ̃ʃ]

chemical weapons	arme (f) chimique	[arm ʃimik]
nuclear (adj)	nucléaire (adj)	[nyklɛɛr]
nuclear weapons	arme (f) nucléaire	[arm nyklɛɛr]

| bomb | bombe (f) | [bɔ̃b] |
| atomic bomb | bombe (f) atomique | [bɔ̃b atɔmik] |

pistol (gun)	pistolet (m)	[pistɔlɛ]
rifle	fusil (m)	[fyzi]
submachine gun	mitraillette (f)	[mitrɑjɛt]
machine gun	mitrailleuse (f)	[mitrɑjøz]

muzzle	bouche (f)	[buʃ]
barrel	canon (m)	[kanɔ̃]
caliber	calibre (m)	[kalibr]

trigger	gâchette (f)	[gaʃɛt]
sight (aiming device)	mire (f)	[mir]
magazine	magasin (m)	[magazɛ̃]
butt (of rifle)	crosse (f)	[krɔs]

| hand grenade | grenade (f) | [grənad] |
| explosive | explosif (m) | [ɛksplozif] |

bullet	balle (f)	[bal]
cartridge	cartouche (f)	[kartuʃ]
charge	charge (f)	[ʃarʒ]
ammunition	munitions (f pl)	[mynisjɔ̃]
bomber (aircraft)	bombardier (m)	[bɔ̃bardje]

| fighter | avion (m) de chasse | [avjɔ̃ də ʃas] |
| helicopter | hélicoptère (m) | [elikɔptɛr] |

anti-aircraft gun	pièce (f) de D.C.A.	[pjɛs də deseɑ]
tank	char (m)	[ʃar]
tank gun	canon (m)	[kanɔ̃]

artillery	artillerie (f)	[artijri]
cannon	canon (m)	[kanɔ̃]
to lay (a gun)	pointer sur ...	[pwɛ̃te syr]

shell (projectile)	obus (m)	[ɔby]
mortar bomb	obus (m) de mortier	[ɔby də mɔrtje]
mortar	mortier (m)	[mɔrtje]
splinter (shell fragment)	éclat (m) d'obus	[ekla dɔby]

submarine	sous-marin (m)	[sumarɛ̃]
torpedo	torpille (f)	[tɔrpij]
missile	missile (m)	[misil]

to load (gun)	charger (vt)	[ʃarʒe]
to shoot (vi)	tirer (vi)	[tire]
to point at (the cannon)	viser (vt)	[vize]
bayonet	baïonnette (f)	[bajɔnɛt]

epee	épée (f)	[epe]
saber (e.g., cavalry ~)	sabre (m)	[sabr]
spear (weapon)	lance (f)	[lɑ̃s]
bow	arc (m)	[ark]
arrow	flèche (f)	[flɛʃ]
musket	mousquet (m)	[muskɛ]
crossbow	arbalète (f)	[arbalɛt]

115. Ancient people

primitive (prehistoric)	primitif (adj)	[primitif]
prehistoric (adj)	préhistorique (adj)	[preistɔrik]
ancient (~ civilization)	ancien (adj)	[ɑ̃sjɛ̃]

Stone Age	Âge (m) de Pierre	[aʒ də pjɛr]
Bronze Age	Âge (m) de Bronze	[aʒ də brɔ̃z]
Ice Age	période (f) glaciaire	[perjɔd glasjɛr]

tribe	tribu (f)	[triby]
cannibal	cannibale (m)	[kanibal]
hunter	chasseur (m)	[ʃasœr]
to hunt (vi, vt)	chasser (vi, vt)	[ʃase]
mammoth	mammouth (m)	[mamut]
cave	caverne (f)	[kavɛrn]
fire	feu (m)	[fø]

| campfire | **feu** (m) **de bois** | [fø də bwa] |
| rock painting | **dessin** (m) **rupestre** | [desɛ̃ rypɛstr] |

tool (e.g., stone ax)	**outil** (m)	[uti]
spear	**lance** (f)	[lɑ̃s]
stone ax	**hache** (f) **en pierre**	[aʃɑ̃ pjɛr]
to be at war	**faire la guerre**	[fɛr la gɛr]
to domesticate (vt)	**domestiquer** (vt)	[dɔmɛstike]

idol	**idole** (f)	[idɔl]
to worship (vt)	**adorer, vénérer** (vt)	[adɔre], [venere]
superstition	**superstition** (f)	[sypɛrstisjɔ̃]
rite	**rite** (m)	[rit]

evolution	**évolution** (f)	[evɔlysjɔ̃]
development	**développement** (m)	[devlɔpmɑ̃]
disappearance (extinction)	**disparition** (f)	[disparisjɔ̃]
to adapt oneself	**s'adapter** (vp)	[sadapte]

archeology	**archéologie** (f)	[arkeɔlɔʒi]
archeologist	**archéologue** (m)	[arkeɔlɔg]
archeological (adj)	**archéologique** (adj)	[arkeɔlɔʒik]

excavation site	**site** (m) **d'excavation**	[sit dɛkskavasjɔ̃]
excavations	**fouilles** (f pl)	[fuj]
find (object)	**trouvaille** (f)	[truvaj]
fragment	**fragment** (m)	[fragmɑ̃]

116. Middle Ages

people (ethnic group)	**peuple** (m)	[pœpl]
peoples	**peuples** (m pl)	[pœpl]
tribe	**tribu** (f)	[triby]
tribes	**tribus** (f pl)	[triby]

barbarians	**Barbares** (m pl)	[barbar]
Gauls	**Gaulois** (m pl)	[golwa]
Goths	**Goths** (m pl)	[go]
Slavs	**Slaves** (m pl)	[slav]
Vikings	**Vikings** (m pl)	[vikiŋ]

| Romans | **Romains** (m pl) | [rɔmɛ̃] |
| Roman (adj) | **romain** (adj) | [rɔmɛ̃] |

Byzantines	**byzantins** (m pl)	[bizɑ̃tɛ̃]
Byzantium	**Byzance** (f)	[bizɑ̃s]
Byzantine (adj)	**byzantin** (adj)	[bizɑ̃tɛ̃]

| emperor | **empereur** (m) | [ɑ̃prœr] |
| leader, chief | **chef** (m) | [ʃɛf] |

powerful (~ king)	**puissant** (adj)	[pɥisɑ̃]
king	**roi** (m)	[rwa]
ruler (sovereign)	**gouverneur** (m)	[guvɛrnœr]
knight	**chevalier** (m)	[ʃəvalje]
feudal lord	**féodal** (m)	[feɔdal]
feudal (adj)	**féodal** (adj)	[feɔdal]
vassal	**vassal** (m)	[vasal]
duke	**duc** (m)	[dyk]
earl	**comte** (m)	[kɔ̃t]
baron	**baron** (m)	[barɔ̃]
bishop	**évêque** (m)	[evɛk]
armor	**armure** (f)	[armyr]
shield	**bouclier** (m)	[buklije]
sword	**épée** (f), **glaive** (m)	[epe], [glɛv]
visor	**visière** (f)	[vizjɛr]
chainmail	**cotte** (f) **de mailles**	[kɔt də maj]
crusade	**croisade** (f)	[krwazad]
crusader	**croisé** (m)	[krwaze]
territory	**territoire** (m)	[tɛritwar]
to attack (invade)	**attaquer** (vt)	[atake]
to conquer (vt)	**conquérir** (vt)	[kɔ̃kerir]
to occupy (invade)	**occuper** (vt)	[ɔkype]
siege (to be under ~)	**siège** (m)	[sjɛʒ]
besieged (adj)	**assiégé** (adj)	[asjeʒe]
to besiege (vt)	**assiéger** (vt)	[asjeʒe]
inquisition	**inquisition** (f)	[ɛ̃kizisjɔ̃]
inquisitor	**inquisiteur** (m)	[ɛ̃kizitœr]
torture	**torture** (f)	[tɔrtyr]
cruel (adj)	**cruel** (adj)	[kryɛl]
heretic	**hérétique** (m)	[eretik]
heresy	**hérésie** (f)	[erezi]
seafaring	**navigation** (f) **en mer**	[navigasjɔn ɑ̃ mɛr]
pirate	**pirate** (m)	[pirat]
piracy	**piraterie** (f)	[piratri]
boarding (attack)	**abordage** (m)	[abɔrdaʒ]
loot, booty	**butin** (m)	[bytɛ̃]
treasures	**trésor** (m)	[trezɔr]
discovery	**découverte** (f)	[dekuvɛrt]
to discover (new land, etc.)	**découvrir** (vt)	[dekuvrir]
expedition	**expédition** (f)	[ɛkspedisjɔ̃]
musketeer	**mousquetaire** (m)	[muskətɛr]
cardinal	**cardinal** (m)	[kardinal]

heraldry	héraldique (f)	[eraldik]
heraldic (adj)	héraldique (adj)	[eraldik]

117. Leader. Chief. Authorities

king	roi (m)	[rwa]
queen	reine (f)	[rɛn]
royal (adj)	royal (adj)	[rwajal]
kingdom	royaume (m)	[rwajom]
prince	prince (m)	[prɛ̃s]
princess	princesse (f)	[prɛ̃sɛs]

president	président (m)	[prezidɑ̃]
vice-president	vice-président (m)	[visprezidɑ̃]
senator	sénateur (m)	[senatœr]

monarch	monarque (m)	[mɔnark]
ruler (sovereign)	gouverneur (m)	[guvɛrnœr]
dictator	dictateur (m)	[diktatœr]
tyrant	tyran (m)	[tirɑ̃]
magnate	magnat (m)	[maɲa]

director	directeur (m)	[dirɛktœr]
chief	chef (m)	[ʃɛf]
manager (director)	gérant (m)	[ʒerɑ̃]
boss	boss (m)	[bɔs]
owner	patron (m)	[patrɔ̃]

leader	leader (m)	[lidœr]
head (~ of delegation)	chef (m)	[ʃɛf]
authorities	autorités (f pl)	[ɔtɔrite]
superiors	supérieurs (m pl)	[syperjœr]

governor	gouverneur (m)	[guvɛrnœr]
consul	consul (m)	[kɔ̃syl]
diplomat	diplomate (m)	[diplɔmat]
mayor	maire (m)	[mɛr]
sheriff	shérif (m)	[ʃerif]

emperor	empereur (m)	[ɑ̃prœr]
tsar, czar	tsar (m)	[tsar]
pharaoh	pharaon (m)	[faraɔ̃]
khan	khan (m)	[kɑ̃]

118. Breaking the law. Criminals. Part 1

bandit	bandit (m)	[bɑ̃di]
crime	crime (m)	[krim]

criminal (person)	**criminel** (m)	[kriminɛl]
thief	**voleur** (m)	[vɔlœr]
to steal (vi, vt)	**voler** (vt)	[vɔle]
stealing, theft	**vol** (m)	[vɔl]

to kidnap (vt)	**kidnapper** (vt)	[kidnape]
kidnapping	**kidnapping** (m)	[kidnapiŋ]
kidnapper	**kidnappeur** (m)	[kidnapœr]

ransom	**rançon** (f)	[rɑ̃sɔ̃]
to demand ransom	**exiger une rançon**	[ɛgziʒe yn rɑ̃sɔ̃]

to rob (vt)	**cambrioler** (vt)	[kɑ̃brijɔle]
robbery	**cambriolage** (m)	[kɑ̃brijɔlaʒ]
robber	**cambrioleur** (m)	[kɑ̃brijɔlœr]

to extort (vt)	**extorquer** (vt)	[ɛkstɔrke]
extortionist	**extorqueur** (m)	[ɛkstɔrkœr]
extortion	**extorsion** (f)	[ɛkstɔrsjɔ̃]

to murder, to kill	**tuer** (vt)	[tɥe]
murder	**meurtre** (m)	[mœrtr]
murderer	**meurtrier** (m)	[mœrtrije]

gunshot	**coup** (m) **de feu**	[ku də fø]
to fire a shot	**tirer un coup de feu**	[tire œ̃ ku də fø]
to shoot to death	**abattre** (vt)	[abatr]
to shoot (vi)	**tirer** (vi)	[tire]
shooting	**coups** (m pl) **de feu**	[ku də fø]

incident (fight, etc.)	**incident** (m)	[ɛ̃sidɑ̃]
fight, brawl	**bagarre** (f)	[bagar]
Help!	**Au secours!**	[osəkur]
victim	**victime** (f)	[viktim]

to damage (vt)	**endommager** (vt)	[ɑ̃dɔmaʒe]
damage	**dommage** (m)	[dɔmaʒ]
dead body	**cadavre** (m)	[kadavr]
grave (~ crime)	**grave** (adj)	[grav]

to attack (vt)	**attaquer** (vt)	[atake]
to beat (dog, person)	**battre** (vt)	[batr]
to beat up	**passer à tabac**	[pɑse ɑ taba]
to take (rob of sth)	**prendre** (vt)	[prɑ̃dr]
to stab to death	**poignarder** (vt)	[pwaɲarde]
to maim (vt)	**mutiler** (vt)	[mytile]
to wound (vt)	**blesser** (vt)	[blese]

blackmail	**chantage** (m)	[ʃɑ̃taʒ]
to blackmail (vt)	**faire chanter**	[fɛr ʃɑ̃te]
blackmailer	**maître** (m) **chanteur**	[mɛtr ʃɑ̃tœr]
protection racket	**racket** (m) **de protection**	[rakɛt də prɔtɛksjɔ̃]

racketeer	racketteur (m)	[rakɛtœr]
gangster	gangster (m)	[gɑ̃gstɛr]
mafia, Mob	mafia (f)	[mafja]

pickpocket	pickpocket (m)	[pikpɔkɛt]
burglar	cambrioleur (m)	[kɑ̃brijɔlœr]
smuggling	contrebande (f)	[kɔ̃trəbɑ̃d]
smuggler	contrebandier (m)	[kɔ̃trebɑ̃dje]

forgery	contrefaçon (f)	[kɔ̃trəfasɔ̃]
to forge (counterfeit)	falsifier (vt)	[falsifje]
fake (forged)	faux (adj)	[fo]

119. Breaking the law. Criminals. Part 2

rape	viol (m)	[vjɔl]
to rape (vt)	violer (vt)	[vjɔle]
rapist	violeur (m)	[vjɔlœr]
maniac	maniaque (m)	[manjak]

prostitute (fem.)	prostituée (f)	[prɔstitɥe]
prostitution	prostitution (f)	[prɔstitysjɔ̃]
pimp	souteneur (m)	[sutnœr]

| drug addict | drogué (m) | [drɔge] |
| drug dealer | trafiquant (m) de drogue | [trafikɑ̃ də drɔg] |

to blow up (bomb)	faire exploser	[fɛr ɛksploze]
explosion	explosion (f)	[ɛksplozjɔ̃]
to set fire	mettre feu	[mɛtr fø]
incendiary (arsonist)	incendiaire (m)	[ɛ̃sɑ̃djɛr]

terrorism	terrorisme (m)	[tɛrɔrism]
terrorist	terroriste (m)	[tɛrɔrist]
hostage	otage (m)	[ɔtaʒ]

to swindle (vt)	escroquer (vt)	[ɛskrɔke]
swindle	escroquerie (f)	[ɛskrɔkri]
swindler	escroc (m)	[ɛskro]

to bribe (vt)	soudoyer (vt)	[sudwaje]
bribery	corruption (f)	[kɔrypsjɔ̃]
bribe	pot-de-vin (m)	[podvɛ̃]

poison	poison (m)	[pwazɔ̃]
to poison (vt)	empoisonner (vt)	[ɑ̃pwazɔne]
to poison oneself	s'empoisonner (vp)	[sɑ̃pwazɔne]

| suicide (act) | suicide (m) | [sɥisid] |
| suicide (person) | suicidé (m) | [sɥiside] |

to threaten (vt)	**menacer** (vt)	[mənase]
threat	**menace** (f)	[mənas]
to make an attempt	**attenter** (vt)	[atɑ̃te]
attempt (attack)	**attentat** (m)	[atɑ̃ta]
to steal (a car)	**voler** (vt)	[vɔle]
to hijack (a plane)	**détourner** (vt)	[deturne]
revenge	**vengeance** (f)	[vɑ̃ʒɑ̃s]
to revenge (vt)	**se venger** (vp)	[sə vɑ̃ʒe]
to torture (vt)	**torturer** (vt)	[tɔrtyre]
torture	**torture** (f)	[tɔrtyr]
to torment (vt)	**tourmenter** (vt)	[turmɑ̃te]
pirate	**pirate** (m)	[pirat]
hooligan	**voyou** (m)	[vwaju]
armed (adj)	**armé** (adj)	[arme]
violence	**violence** (f)	[vjɔlɑ̃s]
illegal (unlawful)	**illégal** (adj)	[ilegal]
spying (n)	**espionnage** (m)	[ɛspjɔnaʒ]
to spy (vi)	**espionner** (vt)	[ɛspjɔne]

120. Police. Law. Part 1

justice	**justice** (f)	[ʒystis]
court (court room)	**tribunal** (m)	[tribynal]
judge	**juge** (m)	[ʒyʒ]
jurors	**jury** (m)	[ʒyri]
jury trial	**cour** (f) **d'assises**	[kur dasiz]
to judge (vt)	**juger** (vt)	[ʒyʒe]
lawyer, attorney	**avocat** (m)	[avɔka]
accused	**accusé** (m)	[akyze]
dock	**banc** (m) **des accusés**	[bɑ̃ dezakyze]
charge	**inculpation** (f)	[ɛ̃kylpasjɔ̃]
accused	**inculpé** (m)	[ɛ̃kylpe]
sentence	**condamnation** (f)	[kɔ̃danasjɔ̃]
to sentence (vt)	**condamner** (vt)	[kɔ̃dane]
guilty (culprit)	**coupable** (m)	[kupabl]
to punish (vt)	**punir** (vt)	[pynir]
punishment	**punition** (f)	[pynisjɔ̃]
fine (penalty)	**amende** (f)	[amɑ̃d]
life imprisonment	**détention** (f) **à vie**	[detɑ̃sjɔ̃ ɑ vi]

death penalty	peine (f) de mort	[pɛn də mɔr]
electric chair	chaise (f) électrique	[ʃɛz elɛktrik]
gallows	potence (f)	[pɔtɑ̃s]

| to execute (vt) | exécuter (vt) | [ɛgzekyte] |
| execution | exécution (f) | [ɛgzekysjɔ̃] |

| prison, jail | prison (f) | [prizɔ̃] |
| cell | cellule (f) | [selyl] |

escort	escorte (f)	[ɛskɔrt]
prison guard	gardien (m) de prison	[gardjɛ̃ də prizɔ̃]
prisoner	prisonnier (m)	[prizɔnje]

| handcuffs | menottes (f pl) | [mənɔt] |
| to handcuff (vt) | mettre les menottes | [mɛtr le mənɔt] |

prison break	évasion (f)	[evazjɔ̃]
to break out (vi)	s'évader (vp)	[sevade]
to disappear (vi)	disparaître (vi)	[disparɛtr]
to release (from prison)	libérer (vt)	[libere]
amnesty	amnistie (f)	[amnisti]

police	police (f)	[pɔlis]
police officer	policier (m)	[pɔlisje]
police station	commissariat (m) de police	[kɔmisarja də pɔlis]

| billy club | matraque (f) | [matrak] |
| bullhorn | haut parleur (m) | [o parlœr] |

patrol car	voiture (f) de patrouille	[vwatyr də patruj]
siren	sirène (f)	[sirɛn]
to turn on the siren	enclencher la sirène	[ɑ̃klɑ̃ʃe la sirɛn]
siren call	hurlement (m) de la sirène	[yrləmɑ̃ dəla sirɛn]

crime scene	lieu (m) du crime	[ljø dy krim]
witness	témoin (m)	[temwɛ̃]
freedom	liberté (f)	[libɛrte]
accomplice	complice (m)	[kɔ̃plis]
to flee (vi)	s'enfuir (vp)	[sɑ̃fɥir]
trace (to leave a ~)	trace (f)	[tras]

121. Police. Law. Part 2

search (investigation)	recherche (f)	[rəʃɛrʃ]
to look for ...	rechercher (vt)	[rəʃɛrʃe]
suspicion	suspicion (f)	[syspisjɔ̃]
suspicious (suspect)	suspect (adj)	[syspɛ]
to stop (cause to halt)	arrêter (vt)	[arete]

to detain (keep in custody)	détenir (vt)	[detnir]
case (lawsuit)	affaire (f)	[afɛr]
investigation	enquête (f)	[ɑ̃kɛt]
detective	détective (m)	[detɛktiv]
investigator	enquêteur (m)	[ɑ̃kɛtœr]
hypothesis	hypothèse (f)	[ipotɛz]
motive	motif (m)	[motif]
interrogation	interrogatoire (m)	[ɛ̃terɔgatwar]
to interrogate (vt)	interroger (vt)	[ɛ̃terɔʒe]
to question (vt)	interroger (vt)	[ɛ̃terɔʒe]
check (identity ~)	inspection (f)	[ɛ̃spɛksjɔ̃]
round-up	rafle (f)	[rafl]
search (~ warrant)	perquisition (f)	[pɛrkizisjɔ̃]
chase (pursuit)	poursuite (f)	[pursɥit]
to pursue, to chase	poursuivre (vt)	[pursɥivr]
to track (a criminal)	dépister (vt)	[depiste]
arrest	arrestation (f)	[arɛstasjɔ̃]
to arrest (sb)	arrêter (vt)	[arete]
to catch (thief, etc.)	attraper (vt)	[atrape]
capture	capture (f)	[kaptyr]
document	document (m)	[dɔkymɑ̃]
proof (evidence)	preuve (f)	[prœv]
to prove (vt)	prouver (vt)	[pruve]
footprint	empreinte (f) de pied	[ɑ̃prɛt də pje]
fingerprints	empreintes (f pl) digitales	[ɑ̃prɛt diʒital]
piece of evidence	élément (m) de preuve	[elemɑ̃ də prœv]
alibi	alibi (m)	[alibi]
innocent (not guilty)	innocent (adj)	[inosɑ̃]
injustice	injustice (f)	[ɛ̃ʒystis]
unjust, unfair (adj)	injuste (adj)	[ɛ̃ʒyst]
criminal (adj)	criminel (adj)	[kriminɛl]
to confiscate (vt)	confisquer (vt)	[kɔ̃fiske]
drug (illegal substance)	drogue (f)	[drɔg]
weapon, gun	arme (f)	[arm]
to disarm (vt)	désarmer (vt)	[dezarme]
to order (command)	ordonner (vt)	[ɔrdɔne]
to disappear (vi)	disparaître (vi)	[disparɛtr]
law	loi (f)	[lwa]
legal, lawful (adj)	légal (adj)	[legal]
illegal, illicit (adj)	illégal (adj)	[ilegal]
responsibility (blame)	responsabilité (f)	[rɛspɔ̃sabilite]
responsible (adj)	responsable (adj)	[rɛspɔ̃sabl]

NATURE

The Earth. Part 1

122. Outer space

cosmos	cosmos (m)	[kɔsmos]
space (as adj)	cosmique (adj)	[kɔsmik]
outer space	espace (m) cosmique	[ɛspas kɔsmik]
world	monde (m)	[mɔ̃d]
universe	univers (m)	[ynivɛr]
galaxy	galaxie (f)	[galaksi]
star	étoile (f)	[etwal]
constellation	constellation (f)	[kɔ̃stelasjɔ̃]
planet	planète (f)	[planɛt]
satellite	satellite (m)	[satelit]
meteorite	météorite (m)	[meteɔrit]
comet	comète (f)	[kɔmɛt]
asteroid	astéroïde (m)	[asterɔid]
orbit	orbite (f)	[ɔrbit]
to revolve	tourner (vi)	[turne]
(~ around the Earth)		
atmosphere	atmosphère (f)	[atmɔsfɛr]
the Sun	Soleil (m)	[sɔlɛj]
solar system	système (m) solaire	[sistɛm sɔlɛr]
solar eclipse	éclipse (f) de soleil	[leklips də sɔlɛj]
the Earth	Terre (f)	[tɛr]
the Moon	Lune (f)	[lyn]
Mars	Mars (m)	[mars]
Venus	Vénus (f)	[venys]
Jupiter	Jupiter (m)	[ʒypitɛr]
Saturn	Saturne (m)	[satyrn]
Mercury	Mercure (m)	[mɛrkyr]
Uranus	Uranus (m)	[yranys]
Neptune	Neptune	[nɛptyn]
Pluto	Pluton (m)	[plytɔ̃]
Milky Way	la Voie Lactée	[la vwa lakte]
Great Bear	la Grande Ours	[la grɑ̃d urs]

North Star	la Polaire	[la pɔlɛr]
Martian	martien (m)	[marsjɛ̃]
extraterrestrial (n)	extraterrestre (m)	[ɛkstratɛrɛstr]
alien	alien (m)	[aljen]
flying saucer	soucoupe (f) volante	[sukup vɔlɑ̃t]

spaceship	vaisseau (m) spatial	[vɛso spasjal]
space station	station (f) orbitale	[stasjɔ̃ ɔrbital]
blast-off	lancement (m)	[lɑ̃smɑ̃]

engine	moteur (m)	[mɔtœr]
nozzle	tuyère (f)	[tyjɛr]
fuel	carburant (m)	[karbyrɑ̃]

cockpit, flight deck	cabine (f)	[kabin]
antenna	antenne (f)	[ɑ̃tɛn]
porthole	hublot (m)	[yblo]
solar battery	batterie (f) solaire	[batri sɔlɛr]
spacesuit	scaphandre (m)	[skafɑ̃dr]

| weightlessness | apesanteur (f) | [apəzɑ̃tœr] |
| oxygen | oxygène (m) | [ɔksiʒɛn] |

| docking (in space) | arrimage (m) | [arimaʒ] |
| to dock (vi, vt) | s'arrimer à ... | [sarime a] |

observatory	observatoire (m)	[ɔpsɛrvatwar]
telescope	télescope (m)	[teleskɔp]
to observe (vt)	observer (vt)	[ɔpsɛrve]
to explore (vt)	explorer (vt)	[ɛksplɔre]

123. The Earth

the Earth	Terre (f)	[tɛr]
globe (the Earth)	globe (m) terrestre	[glɔb tɛrɛstr]
planet	planète (f)	[planɛt]

atmosphere	atmosphère (f)	[atmɔsfɛr]
geography	géographie (f)	[ʒeɔgrafi]
nature	nature (f)	[natyr]

globe (table ~)	globe (m) de table	[glɔb də tabl]
map	carte (f)	[kart]
atlas	atlas (m)	[atlas]

Europe	Europe (f)	[ørɔp]
Asia	Asie (f)	[azi]
Africa	Afrique (f)	[afrik]
Australia	Australie (f)	[ostrali]
America	Amérique (f)	[amerik]

North America	Amérique (f) du Nord	[amerik dy nɔr]
South America	Amérique (f) du Sud	[amerik dy syd]

Antarctica	l'Antarctique (m)	[lɑ̃tarktik]
the Arctic	l'Arctique (m)	[larktik]

124. Cardinal directions

north	nord (m)	[nɔr]
to the north	vers le nord	[vɛr lə nɔr]
in the north	au nord	[onɔr]
northern (adj)	du nord (adj)	[dy nɔr]

south	sud (m)	[syd]
to the south	vers le sud	[vɛr lə syd]
in the south	au sud	[osyd]
southern (adj)	du sud (adj)	[dy syd]

west	ouest (m)	[wɛst]
to the west	vers l'occident	[vɛr lɔksidɑ̃]
in the west	à l'occident	[alɔksidɑ̃]
western (adj)	occidental (adj)	[ɔksidɑ̃tal]

east	est (m)	[ɛst]
to the east	vers l'orient	[vɛr lɔrjɑ̃]
in the east	à l'orient	[alɔrjɑ̃]
eastern (adj)	oriental (adj)	[ɔrjɑ̃tal]

125. Sea. Ocean

sea	mer (f)	[mɛr]
ocean	océan (m)	[ɔseɑ̃]
gulf (bay)	golfe (m)	[gɔlf]
straits	détroit (m)	[detrwa]

solid ground	terre (f) ferme	[tɛr fɛrm]
continent (mainland)	continent (m)	[kɔ̃tinɑ̃]
island	île (f)	[il]
peninsula	presqu'île (f)	[prɛskil]
archipelago	archipel (m)	[arʃipɛl]

bay, cove	baie (f)	[bɛ]
harbor	port (m)	[pɔr]
lagoon	lagune (f)	[lagyn]
cape	cap (m)	[kap]

atoll	atoll (m)	[atɔl]
reef	récif (m)	[resif]

| coral | corail (m) | [kɔraj] |
| coral reef | récif (m) de corail | [resif də kɔraj] |

deep (adj)	profond (adj)	[prɔfɔ̃]
depth (deep water)	profondeur (f)	[prɔfɔ̃dœr]
abyss	abîme (m)	[abim]
trench (e.g., Mariana ~)	fosse (f) océanique	[fos ɔseanik]

| current, stream | courant (m) | [kurɑ̃] |
| to surround (bathe) | baigner (vt) | [beɲe] |

| shore | littoral (m) | [litɔral] |
| coast | côte (f) | [kot] |

high tide	marée (f) haute	[mare ot]
low tide	marée (f) basse	[mare bas]
sandbank	banc (m) de sable	[bɑ̃ də sabl]
bottom	fond (m)	[fɔ̃]

wave	vague (f)	[vag]
crest (~ of a wave)	crête (f) de la vague	[krɛt də la vag]
froth (foam)	mousse (f)	[mus]

storm	tempête (f) en mer	[tɑ̃pɛt ɑ̃mɛr]
hurricane	ouragan (m)	[uragɑ̃]
tsunami	tsunami (m)	[tsynami]
calm (dead ~)	calme (m)	[kalm]
quiet, calm (adj)	calme (adj)	[kalm]

| pole | pôle (m) | [pol] |
| polar (adj) | polaire (adj) | [polɛr] |

latitude	latitude (f)	[latityd]
longitude	longitude (f)	[lɔ̃ʒityd]
parallel	parallèle (f)	[paralɛl]
equator	équateur (m)	[ekwatœr]

sky	ciel (m)	[sjɛl]
horizon	horizon (m)	[ɔrizɔ̃]
air	air (m)	[ɛr]

lighthouse	phare (m)	[far]
to dive (vi)	plonger (vi)	[plɔ̃ʒe]
to sink (ab. boat)	sombrer (vi)	[sɔ̃bre]
treasures	trésor (m)	[trezɔr]

126. Seas' and Oceans' names

| Atlantic Ocean | océan (m) Atlantique | [ɔseɑn atlɑ̃tik] |
| Indian Ocean | océan (m) Indien | [ɔseɑn ɛ̃djɛ̃] |

Pacific Ocean	océan (m) Pacifique	[ɔseã pasifik]
Arctic Ocean	océan (m) Glacial	[ɔseã glasjal]
Black Sea	mer (f) Noire	[mɛr nwar]
Red Sea	mer (f) Rouge	[mɛr ruʒ]
Yellow Sea	mer (f) Jaune	[mɛr ʒon]
White Sea	mer (f) Blanche	[mɛr blãʃ]
Caspian Sea	mer (f) Caspienne	[mɛr kaspjɛn]
Dead Sea	mer (f) Morte	[mɛr mɔrt]
Mediterranean Sea	mer (f) Méditerranée	[mɛr meditɛrane]
Aegean Sea	mer (f) Égée	[mɛr eʒe]
Adriatic Sea	mer (f) Adriatique	[mɛr adrijatik]
Arabian Sea	mer (f) Arabique	[mɛr arabik]
Sea of Japan	mer (f) du Japon	[mɛr dy ʒapɔ̃]
Bering Sea	mer (f) de Béring	[mɛr də beriŋ]
South China Sea	mer (f) de Chine Méridionale	[mɛr də ʃin meridjɔnal]
Coral Sea	mer (f) de Corail	[mɛr də kɔraj]
Tasman Sea	mer (f) de Tasman	[mɛr də tasman]
Caribbean Sea	mer (f) Caraïbe	[mɛr karaib]
Barents Sea	mer (f) de Barents	[mɛr də barɛ̆s]
Kara Sea	mer (f) de Kara	[mɛr də kara]
North Sea	mer (f) du Nord	[mɛr dy nɔr]
Baltic Sea	mer (f) Baltique	[mɛr baltik]
Norwegian Sea	mer (f) de Norvège	[mɛr də nɔrvɛʒ]

127. Mountains

mountain	montagne (f)	[mɔ̃taɲ]
mountain range	chaîne (f) de montagnes	[ʃɛn də mɔ̃taɲ]
mountain ridge	crête (f)	[krɛt]
summit, top	sommet (m)	[sɔmɛ]
peak	pic (m)	[pik]
foot (of mountain)	pied (m)	[pje]
slope (mountainside)	pente (f)	[pãt]
volcano	volcan (m)	[vɔlkã]
active volcano	volcan (m) actif	[vɔlkɑn aktif]
dormant volcano	volcan (m) éteint	[vɔlkɑn etɛ̃]
eruption	éruption (f)	[erypsjɔ̃]
crater	cratère (m)	[kratɛr]

magma	magma (m)	[magma]
lava	lave (f)	[lav]
molten (~ lava)	en fusion	[ɑ̃ fyzjɔ̃]

canyon	canyon (m)	[kanjɔ̃]
gorge	défilé (m)	[defile]
crevice	crevasse (f)	[krəvas]
abyss (chasm)	précipice (m)	[presipis]

pass, col	col (m)	[kɔl]
plateau	plateau (m)	[plato]
cliff	rocher (m)	[rɔʃe]
hill	colline (f)	[kɔlin]

glacier	glacier (m)	[glasje]
waterfall	chute (f) d'eau	[ʃyt do]
geyser	geyser (m)	[ʒɛzɛr]
lake	lac (m)	[lak]

plain	plaine (f)	[plɛn]
landscape	paysage (m)	[peizaʒ]
echo	écho (m)	[eko]

| alpinist | alpiniste (m) | [alpinist] |
| rock climber | varappeur (m) | [varapœr] |

| to conquer (in climbing) | conquérir (vt) | [kɔ̃kerir] |
| climb (an easy ~) | ascension (f) | [asɑ̃sjɔ̃] |

128. Mountains names

Alps	Alpes (f pl)	[alp]
Mont Blanc	Mont Blanc (m)	[mɔ̃blɑ̃]
Pyrenees	Pyrénées (f pl)	[pirene]

| Carpathians | Carpates (f pl) | [karpat] |
| Ural Mountains | Monts Oural (m pl) | [mɔ̃ ural] |

| Caucasus | Caucase (m) | [kokaz] |
| Elbrus | Elbrous (m) | [ɛlbrys] |

Altai	Altaï (m)	[altaj]
Tien Shan	Tian Chan (m)	[tjɑ̃ ʃɑ̃]
Pamir Mountains	Pamir (m)	[pamir]

| Himalayas | Himalaya (m) | [imalaja] |
| Everest | Everest (m) | [evrɛst] |

| Andes | Andes (f pl) | [ɑ̃d] |
| Kilimanjaro | Kilimandjaro (m) | [kilimɑ̃dʒaro] |

129. Rivers

river	rivière (f), fleuve (m)	[rivjɛr], [flœv]
spring (natural source)	source (f)	[surs]
riverbed	lit (m)	[li]
basin	bassin (m)	[basɛ̃]
to flow into ...	se jeter dans ...	[sə ʒəte dɑ̃]
tributary	affluent (m)	[aflyɑ̃]
bank (of river)	rive (f)	[riv]
current, stream	courant (m)	[kurɑ̃]
downstream (adv)	en aval	[ɑn aval]
upstream (adv)	en amont	[ɑn amɔ̃]
inundation	inondation (f)	[inɔ̃dasjɔ̃]
flooding	les grandes crues	[le grɑ̃d kry]
to overflow (vi)	déborder (vt)	[debɔrde]
to flood (vt)	inonder (vt)	[inɔ̃de]
shallows (shoal)	bas-fond (m)	[bafɔ̃]
rapids	rapide (m)	[rapid]
dam	barrage (m)	[baraʒ]
canal	canal (m)	[kanal]
artificial lake	lac (m) de barrage	[lak də baraʒ]
sluice, lock	écluse (f)	[eklyz]
water body (pond, etc.)	plan (m) d'eau	[plɑ̃ do]
swamp, bog	marais (m)	[marɛ]
marsh	fondrière (f)	[fɔ̃drijɛr]
whirlpool	tourbillon (m)	[turbijɔ̃]
stream (brook)	ruisseau (m)	[rɥiso]
drinking (ab. water)	potable (adj)	[pɔtabl]
fresh (~ water)	douce (adj)	[dus]
ice	glace (f)	[glas]
to freeze (ab. river, etc.)	être gelé	[ɛtr ʒəle]

130. Rivers' names

Seine	Seine (f)	[sɛn]
Loire	Loire (f)	[lwar]
Thames	Tamise (f)	[tamiz]
Rhine	Rhin (m)	[rɛ̃]
Danube	Danube (m)	[danyb]
Volga	Volga (f)	[vɔlga]

| Don | **Don** (m) | [dɔ̃] |
| Lena | **Lena** (f) | [lena] |

Yellow River	**Huang He** (m)	[waŋ e]
Yangtze	**Yangzi Jiang** (m)	[jãgzijãg]
Mekong	**Mékong** (m)	[mekɔ̃g]
Ganges	**Gange** (m)	[gãʒ]

Nile River	**Nil** (m)	[nil]
Congo	**Congo** (m)	[kɔ̃go]
Okavango	**Okavango** (m)	[ɔkavangɔ]
Zambezi	**Zambèze** (m)	[zãbɛz]
Limpopo	**Limpopo** (m)	[limpɔpo]
Mississippi River	**Mississippi** (m)	[misisipi]

131. Forest

| forest | **forêt** (f) | [fɔrɛ] |
| forest (as adj) | **forestier** (adj) | [fɔrɛstje] |

thick forest	**fourré** (m)	[fure]
grove	**bosquet** (m)	[bɔskɛ]
forest clearing	**clairière** (f)	[klɛrjɛr]

| thicket | **broussailles** (f pl) | [brusaj] |
| scrubland | **taillis** (m) | [taji] |

| footpath (troddenpath) | **sentier** (m) | [sãtje] |
| gully | **ravin** (m) | [ravɛ̃] |

tree	**arbre** (m)	[arbr]
leaf	**feuille** (f)	[fœj]
leaves	**feuillage** (m)	[fœjaʒ]

fall of leaves	**chute** (f) **de feuilles**	[ʃyt də fœj]
to fall (ab. leaves)	**tomber** (vi)	[tɔ̃be]
top (of the tree)	**sommet** (m)	[sɔmɛ]

branch	**rameau** (m)	[ramo]
bough	**branche** (f)	[brãʃ]
bud (on shrub, tree)	**bourgeon** (m)	[burʒɔ̃]
needle (of pine tree)	**aiguille** (f)	[eguij]
pine cone	**pomme** (f) **de pin**	[pɔm də pɛ̃]

hollow (in a tree)	**creux** (m)	[krø]
nest	**nid** (m)	[ni]
burrow (animal hole)	**terrier** (m)	[tɛrje]

| trunk | **tronc** (m) | [trɔ̃] |
| root | **racine** (f) | [rasin] |

| bark | écorce (f) | [ekɔrs] |
| moss | mousse (f) | [mus] |

to uproot (vt)	déraciner (vt)	[derasine]
to chop down	abattre (vt)	[abatr]
to deforest (vt)	déboiser (vt)	[debwaze]
tree stump	souche (f)	[suʃ]

campfire	feu (m) de bois	[fø də bwa]
forest fire	incendie (m)	[ɛ̃sɑ̃di]
to extinguish (vt)	éteindre (vt)	[etɛ̃dr]

forest ranger	garde (m) forestier	[gard fɔrɛstje]
protection	protection (f)	[prɔtɛksjɔ̃]
to protect (~ nature)	protéger (vt)	[prɔteʒe]
poacher	braconnier (m)	[brakɔnje]
trap (e.g., bear ~)	piège (m) à mâchoires	[pjɛʒ a mɑʃwar]

| to gather, to pick (vt) | cueillir (vt) | [kœjir] |
| to lose one's way | s'égarer (vp) | [segare] |

132. Natural resources

natural resources	ressources (f pl) naturelles	[rəsurs natyrɛl]
minerals	minéraux (m pl)	[minero]
deposits	gisement (m)	[ʒizmɑ̃]
field (e.g., oilfield)	champ (m)	[ʃɑ̃]

to mine (extract)	extraire (vt)	[ɛkstrɛr]
mining (extraction)	extraction (f)	[ɛkstraksjɔ̃]
ore	minerai (m)	[minrɛ]
mine (e.g., for coal)	mine (f)	[min]
mine shaft, pit	puits (m) de mine	[pɥi də min]
miner	mineur (m)	[minœr]

| gas | gaz (m) | [gaz] |
| gas pipeline | gazoduc (m) | [gazɔdyk] |

oil (petroleum)	pétrole (m)	[petrɔl]
oil pipeline	pipeline (m)	[piplin]
oil well	tour (f) de forage	[tur də fɔraʒ]
derrick	derrick (m)	[derik]
tanker	pétrolier (m)	[petrɔlje]

sand	sable (m)	[sabl]
limestone	calcaire (m)	[kalkɛr]
gravel	gravier (m)	[gravje]
peat	tourbe (f)	[turb]
clay	argile (f)	[arʒil]

coal	charbon (m)	[ʃarbɔ̃]
iron	fer (m)	[fɛr]
gold	or (m)	[ɔr]
silver	argent (m)	[arʒɑ̃]
nickel	nickel (m)	[nikɛl]
copper	cuivre (m)	[kɥivr]

zinc	zinc (m)	[zɛ̃g]
manganese	manganèse (m)	[mɑ̃ganɛz]
mercury	mercure (m)	[mɛrkyr]
lead	plomb (m)	[plɔ̃]

mineral	minéral (m)	[mineral]
crystal	cristal (m)	[kristal]
marble	marbre (m)	[marbr]
uranium	uranium (m)	[yranjɔm]

The Earth. Part 2

133. Weather

weather	**temps** (m)	[tɑ̃]
weather forecast	**météo** (f)	[meteo]
temperature	**température** (f)	[tɑ̃peratyr]
thermometer	**thermomètre** (m)	[tɛrmɔmɛtr]
barometer	**baromètre** (m)	[barɔmɛtr]
humid (adj)	**humide** (adj)	[ymid]
humidity	**humidité** (f)	[ymidite]
heat (extreme ~)	**chaleur** (f)	[ʃalœr]
hot (torrid)	**torride** (adj)	[tɔrid]
it's hot	**il fait très chaud**	[il fɛ trɛ ʃo]
it's warm	**il fait chaud**	[il fɛʃo]
warm (moderately hot)	**chaud** (adj)	[ʃo]
it's cold	**il fait froid**	[il fɛ frwa]
cold (adj)	**froid** (adj)	[frwa]
sun	**soleil** (m)	[sɔlɛj]
to shine (vi)	**briller** (vi)	[brije]
sunny (day)	**ensoleillé** (adj)	[ɑ̃sɔleje]
to come up (vi)	**se lever** (vp)	[sə ləve]
to set (vi)	**se coucher** (vp)	[sə kuʃe]
cloud	**nuage** (m)	[nɥaʒ]
cloudy (adj)	**nuageux** (adj)	[nɥaʒø]
rain cloud	**nuée** (f)	[nɥe]
somber (gloomy)	**sombre** (adj)	[sɔ̃br]
rain	**pluie** (f)	[plɥi]
it's raining	**il pleut**	[il plø]
rainy (day)	**pluvieux** (adj)	[plyvjø]
to drizzle (vi)	**bruiner** (v imp)	[brɥine]
pouring rain	**pluie** (f) **torrentielle**	[plɥi tɔrɑ̃sjɛl]
downpour	**averse** (f)	[avɛrs]
heavy (e.g., ~ rain)	**forte** (adj)	[fɔrt]
puddle	**flaque** (f)	[flak]
to get wet (in rain)	**se faire mouiller**	[sə fɛr muje]
fog (mist)	**brouillard** (m)	[brujar]
foggy	**brumeux** (adj)	[brymø]

| snow | **neige** (f) | [nεʒ] |
| it's snowing | **il neige** | [il nεʒ] |

134. Severe weather. Natural disasters

thunderstorm	**orage** (m)	[ɔraʒ]
lightning (~ strike)	**éclair** (m)	[eklεr]
to flash (vi)	**éclater** (vi)	[eklate]

thunder	**tonnerre** (m)	[tɔnεr]
to thunder (vi)	**gronder** (vi)	[grɔ̃de]
it's thundering	**le tonnerre gronde**	[lə tɔnεr grɔ̃d]

| hail | **grêle** (f) | [grεl] |
| it's hailing | **il grêle** | [il grεl] |

| to flood (vt) | **inonder** (vt) | [inɔ̃de] |
| flood, inundation | **inondation** (f) | [inɔ̃dasjɔ̃] |

earthquake	**tremblement** (m) **de terre**	[trɑ̃bləmɑ̃ də tεr]
tremor, quake	**secousse** (f)	[səkus]
epicenter	**épicentre** (m)	[episɑ̃tr]

| eruption | **éruption** (f) | [erypsjɔ̃] |
| lava | **lave** (f) | [lav] |

twister	**tourbillon** (m)	[turbijɔ̃]
tornado	**tornade** (f)	[tɔrnad]
typhoon	**typhon** (m)	[tifɔ̃]

hurricane	**ouragan** (m)	[uragɑ̃]
storm	**tempête** (f)	[tɑ̃pεt]
tsunami	**tsunami** (m)	[tsynami]

cyclone	**cyclone** (m)	[siklon]
bad weather	**intempéries** (f pl)	[ε̃tɑ̃peri]
fire (accident)	**incendie** (m)	[ε̃sɑ̃di]
disaster	**catastrophe** (f)	[katastrɔf]
meteorite	**météorite** (m)	[meteɔrit]

avalanche	**avalanche** (f)	[avalɑ̃ʃ]
snowslide	**éboulement** (m)	[ebulmɑ̃]
blizzard	**blizzard** (m)	[blizar]
snowstorm	**tempête** (f) **de neige**	[tɑ̃pεt də nεʒ]

Fauna

135. Mammals. Predators

predator	prédateur (m)	[predatœr]
tiger	tigre (m)	[tigr]
lion	lion (m)	[ljɔ̃]
wolf	loup (m)	[lu]
fox	renard (m)	[rənar]

jaguar	jaguar (m)	[ʒagwar]
leopard	léopard (m)	[leɔpar]
cheetah	guépard (m)	[gepar]

black panther	panthère (f)	[pɑ̃tɛr]
puma	puma (m)	[pyma]
snow leopard	léopard (m) de neiges	[leɔpar də nɛʒ]
lynx	lynx (m)	[lɛ̃ks]

coyote	coyote (m)	[kɔjɔt]
jackal	chacal (m)	[ʃakal]
hyena	hyène (f)	[jɛn]

136. Wild animals

| animal | animal (m) | [animal] |
| beast (animal) | bête (f) | [bɛt] |

squirrel	écureuil (m)	[ekyrœj]
hedgehog	hérisson (m)	[erisɔ̃]
hare	lièvre (m)	[ljɛvr]
rabbit	lapin (m)	[lapɛ̃]

badger	blaireau (m)	[blɛro]
raccoon	raton (m)	[ratɔ̃]
hamster	hamster (m)	[amstɛr]
marmot	marmotte (f)	[marmɔt]

mole	taupe (f)	[top]
mouse	souris (f)	[suri]
rat	rat (m)	[ra]
bat	chauve-souris (f)	[ʃovsuri]
ermine	hermine (f)	[ɛrmin]
sable	zibeline (f)	[ziblin]

marten	martre (f)	[martr]
weasel	belette (f)	[bəlɛt]
mink	vison (m)	[vizɔ̃]

| beaver | castor (m) | [kastɔr] |
| otter | loutre (f) | [lutr] |

horse	cheval (m)	[ʃəval]
moose	élan (m)	[elɑ̃]
deer	cerf (m)	[sɛr]
camel	chameau (m)	[ʃamo]

bison	bison (m)	[bizɔ̃]
aurochs	aurochs (m)	[orɔk]
buffalo	buffle (m)	[byfl]

zebra	zèbre (m)	[zɛbr]
antelope	antilope (f)	[ɑ̃tilɔp]
roe deer	chevreuil (m)	[ʃəvrœj]
fallow deer	biche (f)	[biʃ]
chamois	chamois (m)	[ʃamwa]
wild boar	sanglier (m)	[sɑ̃glije]

whale	baleine (f)	[balɛn]
seal	phoque (m)	[fɔk]
walrus	morse (m)	[mɔrs]
fur seal	ours (m) de mer	[urs də mɛr]
dolphin	dauphin (m)	[dofɛ̃]

bear	ours (m)	[urs]
polar bear	ours (m) blanc	[urs blɑ̃]
panda	panda (m)	[pɑ̃da]

monkey	singe (m)	[sɛ̃ʒ]
chimpanzee	chimpanzé (m)	[ʃɛ̃pɑ̃ze]
orangutan	orang-outang (m)	[ɔrɑ̃utɑ̃]
gorilla	gorille (m)	[gɔrij]
macaque	macaque (m)	[makak]
gibbon	gibbon (m)	[ʒibɔ̃]

elephant	éléphant (m)	[elefɑ̃]
rhinoceros	rhinocéros (m)	[rinɔserɔs]
giraffe	girafe (f)	[ʒiraf]
hippopotamus	hippopotame (m)	[ipɔpɔtam]

| kangaroo | kangourou (m) | [kɑ̃guru] |
| koala (bear) | koala (m) | [kɔala] |

mongoose	mangouste (f)	[mɑ̃gust]
chinchilla	chinchilla (m)	[ʃɛ̃ʃila]
skunk	mouffette (f)	[mufɛt]
porcupine	porc-épic (m)	[pɔrkepik]

137. Domestic animals

cat	chat (m)	[ʃa]
tomcat	chat (m)	[ʃa]
dog	chien (m)	[ʃjɛ̃]

horse	cheval (m)	[ʃəval]
stallion	étalon (m)	[etalɔ̃]
mare	jument (f)	[ʒymɑ̃]

cow	vache (f)	[vaʃ]
bull	taureau (m)	[tɔro]
ox	bœuf (m)	[bœf]

sheep	brebis (f)	[brəbi]
ram	mouton (m)	[mutɔ̃]
goat	chèvre (f)	[ʃɛvr]
billy goat, he-goat	bouc (m)	[buk]

| donkey | âne (m) | [ɑn] |
| mule | mulet (m) | [mylɛ] |

pig	cochon (m)	[kɔʃɔ̃]
piglet	pourceau (m)	[purso]
rabbit	lapin (m)	[lapɛ̃]
hen (chicken)	poule (f)	[pul]
rooster	coq (m)	[kɔk]

duck	canard (m)	[kanar]
drake	canard (m) mâle	[kanar mal]
goose	oie (f)	[wa]

| tom turkey | dindon (m) | [dɛ̃dɔ̃] |
| turkey (hen) | dinde (f) | [dɛ̃d] |

domestic animals	animaux (m pl) domestiques	[animo dɔmɛstik]
tame (e.g., ~ hamster)	apprivoisé (adj)	[aprivwaze]
to tame (vt)	apprivoiser (vt)	[aprivwaze]
to breed (vt)	élever (vt)	[elve]

farm	ferme (f)	[fɛrm]
poultry	volaille (f)	[vɔlaj]
cattle	bétail (m)	[betaj]
herd (cattle)	troupeau (m)	[trupo]

stable	écurie (f)	[ekyri]
pigsty	porcherie (f)	[pɔrʃəri]
cowshed	vacherie (f)	[vaʃri]
rabbit hutch	cabane (f) à lapins	[kaban ɑ lapɛ̃]
hen house	poulailler (m)	[pulaje]

138. Birds

bird	oiseau (m)	[wazo]
pigeon	pigeon (m)	[piʒɔ̃]
sparrow	moineau (m)	[mwano]
tit	mésange (f)	[mezɑ̃ʒ]
magpie	pie (f)	[pi]
raven	corbeau (m)	[kɔrbo]
crow	corneille (f)	[kɔrnɛj]
jackdaw	choucas (m)	[ʃuka]
rook	freux (m)	[frø]
duck	canard (m)	[kanar]
goose	oie (f)	[wa]
pheasant	faisan (m)	[fəzɑ̃]
eagle	aigle (m)	[ɛgl]
hawk	épervier (m)	[epɛrvje]
falcon	faucon (m)	[fokɔ̃]
vulture	vautour (m)	[votur]
condor (Andean ~)	condor (m)	[kɔ̃dɔr]
swan	cygne (m)	[siɲ]
crane	grue (f)	[gry]
stork	cigogne (f)	[sigɔɲ]
parrot	perroquet (m)	[perɔkɛ]
hummingbird	colibri (m)	[kɔlibri]
peacock	paon (m)	[pɑ̃]
ostrich	autruche (f)	[otryʃ]
heron	héron (m)	[erɔ̃]
flamingo	flamant (m)	[flamɑ̃]
pelican	pélican (m)	[pelikɑ̃]
nightingale	rossignol (m)	[rɔsiɲɔl]
swallow	hirondelle (f)	[irɔ̃dɛl]
thrush	merle (m)	[mɛrl]
song thrush	grive (f)	[griv]
blackbird	merle (m) noir	[mɛrl nwar]
swift	martinet (m)	[martinɛ]
lark	alouette (f) des champs	[alwɛt de ʃɑ̃]
quail	caille (f)	[kaj]
woodpecker	pivert (m)	[pivɛr]
cuckoo	coucou (m)	[kuku]
owl	chouette (f)	[ʃwɛt]
eagle owl	hibou (m)	[ibu]

wood grouse	tétras (m)	[tetra]
black grouse	tétras-lyre (m)	[tetralir]
partridge	perdrix (f)	[pɛrdri]

starling	étourneau (m)	[eturno]
canary	canari (m)	[kanari]
hazel grouse	gélinotte (f) des bois	[ʒelinɔt də bwa]
chaffinch	pinson (m)	[pɛ̃sɔ̃]
bullfinch	bouvreuil (m)	[buvrœj]

seagull	mouette (f)	[mwɛt]
albatross	albatros (m)	[albatros]
penguin	pingouin (m)	[pɛ̃gwɛ̃]

139. Fish. Marine animals

bream	brème (f)	[brɛm]
carp	carpe (f)	[karp]
perch	perche (f)	[pɛrʃ]
catfish	silure (m)	[silyr]
pike	brochet (m)	[brɔʃɛ]

| salmon | saumon (m) | [somɔ̃] |
| sturgeon | esturgeon (m) | [ɛstyrʒɔ̃] |

herring	hareng (m)	[arɑ̃]
Atlantic salmon	saumon (m) atlantique	[somɔ̃ atlɑ̃tik]
mackerel	maquereau (m)	[makro]
flatfish	flet (m)	[flɛ]

zander, pike perch	sandre (f)	[sɑ̃dr]
cod	morue (f)	[mɔry]
tuna	thon (m)	[tɔ̃]
trout	truite (f)	[trɥit]

eel	anguille (f)	[ɑ̃gij]
electric ray	torpille (f)	[tɔrpij]
moray eel	murène (f)	[myrɛn]
piranha	piranha (m)	[piraɲa]

shark	requin (m)	[rəkɛ̃]
dolphin	dauphin (m)	[dofɛ̃]
whale	baleine (f)	[balɛn]

crab	crabe (m)	[krab]
jellyfish	méduse (f)	[medyz]
octopus	pieuvre (f), poulpe (m)	[pjœvr], [pulp]

| starfish | étoile (f) de mer | [etwal də mɛr] |
| sea urchin | oursin (m) | [ursɛ̃] |

seahorse	hippocampe (m)	[ipɔkɑ̃p]
oyster	huître (f)	[ɥitr]
shrimp	crevette (f)	[krəvɛt]
lobster	homard (m)	[ɔmar]
spiny lobster	langoustine (f)	[lɑ̃gustin]

140. Amphibians. Reptiles

| snake | serpent (m) | [sɛrpɑ̃] |
| venomous (snake) | venimeux (adj) | [vənimø] |

viper	vipère (f)	[vipɛr]
cobra	cobra (m)	[kɔbra]
python	python (m)	[pitɔ̃]
boa	boa (m)	[bɔa]

grass snake	couleuvre (f)	[kulœvr]
rattle snake	serpent (m) à sonnettes	[sɛrpɑ̃ ɑ sɔnɛt]
anaconda	anaconda (m)	[anakɔ̃da]

lizard	lézard (m)	[lezar]
iguana	iguane (m)	[igwan]
monitor lizard	varan (m)	[varɑ̃]
salamander	salamandre (f)	[salamɑ̃dr]
chameleon	caméléon (m)	[kameleɔ̃]
scorpion	scorpion (m)	[skɔrpjɔ̃]

turtle	tortue (f)	[tɔrty]
frog	grenouille (f)	[grənuj]
toad	crapaud (m)	[krapo]
crocodile	crocodile (m)	[krɔkɔdil]

141. Insects

insect, bug	insecte (m)	[ɛ̃sɛkt]
butterfly	papillon (m)	[papijɔ̃]
ant	fourmi (f)	[furmi]
fly	mouche (f)	[muʃ]
mosquito	moustique (m)	[mustik]
beetle	scarabée (m)	[skarabe]

wasp	guêpe (f)	[gɛp]
bee	abeille (f)	[abɛj]
bumblebee	bourdon (m)	[burdɔ̃]
gadfly	œstre (m)	[ɛstr]

| spider | araignée (f) | [areɲe] |
| spider's web | toile (f) d'araignée | [twal dareɲe] |

dragonfly	**libellule** (f)	[libelyl]
grasshopper	**sauterelle** (f)	[sotrɛl]
moth (night butterfly)	**papillon** (m)	[papijɔ̃]
cockroach	**cafard** (m)	[kafar]
tick	**tique** (f)	[tik]
flea	**puce** (f)	[pys]
midge	**moucheron** (m)	[muʃrɔ̃]
locust	**criquet** (m)	[krikɛ]
snail	**escargot** (m)	[ɛskargo]
cricket	**grillon** (m)	[grijɔ̃]
lightning bug	**luciole** (f)	[lysjɔl]
ladybug	**coccinelle** (f)	[kɔksinɛl]
cockchafer	**hanneton** (m)	[antɔ̃]
leech	**sangsue** (f)	[sɑ̃sy]
caterpillar	**chenille** (f)	[ʃənij]
earthworm	**ver** (m)	[vɛr]
larva	**larve** (f)	[larv]

Flora

142. Trees

tree	**arbre** (m)	[arbr]
deciduous (adj)	**à feuilles caduques**	[ɑ fœj kadyk]
coniferous (adj)	**conifère** (adj)	[kɔnifɛr]
evergreen (adj)	**à feuilles persistantes**	[a fœj pɛrsistɑ̃t]
apple tree	**pommier** (m)	[pɔmje]
pear tree	**poirier** (m)	[pwarje]
sweet cherry tree	**merisier** (m)	[mərizje]
sour cherry tree	**cerisier** (m)	[sərizje]
plum tree	**prunier** (m)	[prynje]
birch	**bouleau** (m)	[bulo]
oak	**chêne** (m)	[ʃɛn]
linden tree	**tilleul** (m)	[tijœl]
aspen	**tremble** (m)	[trɑ̃bl]
maple	**érable** (m)	[erabl]
spruce	**épicéa** (m)	[episea]
pine	**pin** (m)	[pɛ̃]
larch	**mélèze** (m)	[melɛz]
fir tree	**sapin** (m)	[sapɛ̃]
cedar	**cèdre** (m)	[sɛdr]
poplar	**peuplier** (m)	[pøplije]
rowan	**sorbier** (m)	[sɔrbje]
willow	**saule** (m)	[sol]
alder	**aune** (m)	[on]
beech	**hêtre** (m)	[ɛtr]
elm	**orme** (m)	[ɔrm]
ash (tree)	**frêne** (m)	[frɛn]
chestnut	**marronnier** (m)	[marɔnje]
magnolia	**magnolia** (m)	[maɲɔlja]
palm tree	**palmier** (m)	[palmje]
cypress	**cyprès** (m)	[siprɛ]
mangrove	**palétuvier** (m)	[paletyvje]
baobab	**baobab** (m)	[baɔbab]
eucalyptus	**eucalyptus** (m)	[økaliptys]
sequoia	**séquoia** (m)	[sekɔja]

143. Shrubs

bush	buisson (m)	[bɥisɔ̃]
shrub	arbrisseau (m)	[arbriso]
grapevine	vigne (f)	[viɲ]
vineyard	vigne (f)	[viɲ]
raspberry bush	framboise (f)	[frãbwaz]
blackcurrant bush	cassis (m)	[kasis]
redcurrant bush	groseille (f) rouge	[grozɛj ruʒ]
gooseberry bush	groseille (f) verte	[grozɛj vɛrt]
acacia	acacia (m)	[akasja]
barberry	berbéris (m)	[bɛrberis]
jasmine	jasmin (m)	[ʒasmɛ̃]
juniper	genévrier (m)	[ʒənevrije]
rosebush	rosier (m)	[rozje]
dog rose	églantier (m)	[eglãtje]

144. Fruits. Berries

fruit	fruit (m)	[frɥi]
fruits	fruits (m pl)	[frɥi]
apple	pomme (f)	[pɔm]
pear	poire (f)	[pwar]
plum	prune (f)	[pryn]
strawberry	fraise (f)	[frɛz]
sour cherry	cerise (f)	[səriz]
sweet cherry	merise (f)	[məriz]
grape	raisin (m)	[rɛzɛ̃]
raspberry	framboise (f)	[frãbwaz]
blackcurrant	cassis (m)	[kasis]
redcurrant	groseille (f) rouge	[grozɛj ruʒ]
gooseberry	groseille (f) verte	[grozɛj vɛrt]
cranberry	canneberge (f)	[kanbɛrʒ]
orange	orange (f)	[ɔrãʒ]
mandarin	mandarine (f)	[mãdarin]
pineapple	ananas (m)	[anana]
banana	banane (f)	[banan]
date	datte (f)	[dat]
lemon	citron (m)	[sitrɔ̃]
apricot	abricot (m)	[abriko]
peach	pêche (f)	[pɛʃ]

kiwi	**kiwi** (m)	[kiwi]
grapefruit	**pamplemousse** (m)	[pɑ̃pləmus]
berry	**baie** (f)	[bɛ]
berries	**baies** (f pl)	[bɛ]
cowberry	**airelle** (f) **rouge**	[ɛrɛl ruʒ]
field strawberry	**fraise** (f) **des bois**	[frɛz de bwa]
bilberry	**myrtille** (f)	[mirtij]

145. Flowers. Plants

flower	**fleur** (f)	[flœr]
bouquet (of flowers)	**bouquet** (m)	[bukɛ]
rose (flower)	**rose** (f)	[roz]
tulip	**tulipe** (f)	[tylip]
carnation	**oeillet** (m)	[œjɛ]
gladiolus	**glaïeul** (m)	[glajœl]
cornflower	**bleuet** (m)	[bløɛ]
bluebell	**campanule** (f)	[kɑ̃panyl]
dandelion	**dent-de-lion** (f)	[dɑ̃dəljɔ̃]
camomile	**marguerite** (f)	[margərit]
aloe	**aloès** (m)	[alɔɛs]
cactus	**cactus** (m)	[kaktys]
rubber plant, ficus	**ficus** (m)	[fikys]
lily	**lis** (m)	[li]
geranium	**géranium** (m)	[ʒeranjɔm]
hyacinth	**jacinthe** (f)	[ʒasɛ̃t]
mimosa	**mimosa** (m)	[mimɔza]
narcissus	**jonquille** (f)	[ʒɔ̃kij]
nasturtium	**capucine** (f)	[kapysin]
orchid	**orchidée** (f)	[ɔrkide]
peony	**pivoine** (f)	[pivwan]
violet	**violette** (f)	[vjɔlɛt]
pansy	**pensée** (f)	[pɑ̃se]
forget-me-not	**myosotis** (m)	[mjɔzɔtis]
daisy	**pâquerette** (f)	[pɑkrɛt]
poppy	**coquelicot** (m)	[kɔkliko]
hemp	**chanvre** (m)	[ʃɑ̃vr]
mint	**menthe** (f)	[mɑ̃t]
lily of the valley	**muguet** (m)	[mygɛ]
snowdrop	**perce-neige** (f)	[pɛrsənɛʒ]

nettle	**ortie** (f)	[ɔrti]
sorrel	**oseille** (f)	[ozɛj]
water lily	**nénuphar** (m)	[nenyfar]
fern	**fougère** (f)	[fuʒɛr]
lichen	**lichen** (m)	[likɛn]
tropical greenhouse	**serre** (f) **tropicale**	[sɛr trɔpikal]
grass lawn	**gazon** (m)	[gazɔ̃]
flowerbed	**parterre** (m) **de fleurs**	[partɛr də flœr]
plant	**plante** (f)	[plɑ̃t]
grass, herb	**herbe** (f)	[ɛrb]
blade of grass	**brin** (m) **d'herbe**	[brɛ̃ dɛrb]
leaf	**feuille** (f)	[fœj]
petal	**pétale** (m)	[petal]
stem	**tige** (f)	[tiʒ]
tuber	**tubercule** (m)	[tybɛrkyl]
young plant (shoot)	**pousse** (f)	[pus]
thorn	**épine** (f)	[epin]
to blossom (vi)	**fleurir** (vi)	[flœrir]
to fade, to wither	**se faner** (vp)	[sə fane]
smell (odor)	**odeur** (f)	[ɔdœr]
to cut (flowers)	**couper** (vt)	[kupe]
to pick (a flower)	**cueillir** (vt)	[kœjir]

146. Cereals, grains

grain	**grains** (m pl)	[grɛ̃]
cereal crops	**céréales** (f pl)	[sereal]
ear (of barley, etc.)	**épi** (m)	[epi]
wheat	**blé** (m)	[ble]
rye	**seigle** (m)	[sɛgl]
oats	**avoine** (f)	[avwan]
millet	**millet** (m)	[mijɛ]
barley	**orge** (f)	[ɔrʒ]
corn	**maïs** (m)	[mais]
rice	**riz** (m)	[ri]
buckwheat	**sarrasin** (m)	[sarazɛ̃]
pea plant	**pois** (m)	[pwa]
kidney bean	**haricot** (m)	[ariko]
soy	**soja** (m)	[sɔʒa]
lentil	**lentille** (f)	[lɑ̃tij]

COUNTRIES. NATIONALITIES

147. Western Europe

Europe	Europe (f)	[ørɔp]
European Union	Union (f) européenne	[ynjɔn ørɔpeɛn]
Austria	Autriche (f)	[otriʃ]
Great Britain	Grande-Bretagne (f)	[grãdbrətaɲ]
England	Angleterre (f)	[ãglətɛr]
Belgium	Belgique (f)	[bɛlʒik]
Germany	Allemagne (f)	[almaɲ]
Netherlands	Pays-Bas (m)	[peiba]
Holland	Hollande (f)	[ɔlãd]
Greece	Grèce (f)	[grɛs]
Denmark	Danemark (m)	[danmark]
Ireland	Irlande (f)	[irlãd]
Iceland	Islande (f)	[islãd]
Spain	Espagne (f)	[ɛspaɲ]
Italy	Italie (f)	[itali]
Cyprus	Chypre (m)	[ʃipr]
Malta	Malte (f)	[malt]
Norway	Norvège (f)	[nɔrvɛʒ]
Portugal	Portugal (m)	[pɔrtygal]
Finland	Finlande (f)	[fɛ̃lãd]
France	France (f)	[frãs]
Sweden	Suède (f)	[sɥɛd]
Switzerland	Suisse (f)	[sɥis]
Scotland	Écosse (f)	[ekɔs]
Vatican	Vatican (m)	[vatikã]
Liechtenstein	Liechtenstein (m)	[liʃtɛnʃtajn]
Luxembourg	Luxembourg (m)	[lyksãbur]
Monaco	Monaco (m)	[mɔnako]

148. Central and Eastern Europe

Albania	Albanie (f)	[albani]
Bulgaria	Bulgarie (f)	[bylgari]
Hungary	Hongrie (f)	[õgri]

Latvia	Lettonie (f)	[lɛtɔni]
Lithuania	Lituanie (f)	[lituani]
Poland	Pologne (f)	[pɔlɔɲ]

Romania	Roumanie (f)	[rumani]
Serbia	Serbie (f)	[sɛrbi]
Slovakia	Slovaquie (f)	[slɔvaki]

Croatia	Croatie (f)	[krɔasi]
Czech Republic	République (f) Tchèque	[repyblik tʃɛk]
Estonia	Estonie (f)	[ɛstɔni]

Bosnia-Herzegovina	Bosnie (f)	[bɔsni]
Macedonia	Macédoine (f)	[masedwan]
Slovenia	Slovénie (f)	[slɔveni]
Montenegro	Monténégro (m)	[mɔ̃tenegro]

149. Former USSR countries

| Azerbaijan | Azerbaïdjan (m) | [azɛrbajdʒɑ̃] |
| Armenia | Arménie (f) | [armeni] |

Belarus	Biélorussie (f)	[bjelɔrysi]
Georgia	Géorgie (f)	[ʒeɔrʒi]
Kazakhstan	Kazakhstan (m)	[kazakstɑ̃]
Kirghizia	Kirghizistan (m)	[kirgizistɑ̃]
Moldavia	Moldavie (f)	[mɔldavi]

| Russia | Russie (f) | [rysi] |
| Ukraine | Ukraine (f) | [ykrɛn] |

Tajikistan	Tadjikistan (m)	[tadʒikistɑ̃]
Turkmenistan	Turkménistan (m)	[tyrkmenistɑ̃]
Uzbekistan	Ouzbékistan (m)	[uzbekistɑ̃]

150. Asia

Asia	Asie (f)	[azi]
Vietnam	Vietnam (m)	[vjɛtnam]
India	Inde (f)	[ɛ̃d]
Israel	Israël (m)	[israɛl]

China	Chine (f)	[ʃin]
Lebanon	Liban (m)	[libɑ̃]
Mongolia	Mongolie (f)	[mɔ̃gɔli]

| Malaysia | Malaisie (f) | [malɛzi] |
| Pakistan | Pakistan (m) | [pakistɑ̃] |

Saudi Arabia	**Arabie** (f) **Saoudite**	[arabi saudit]
Thailand	**Thaïlande** (f)	[tajlɑ̃d]
Taiwan	**Taïwan** (m)	[tajwan]
Turkey	**Turquie** (f)	[tyrki]
Japan	**Japon** (m)	[ʒapɔ̃]

Afghanistan	**Afghanistan** (m)	[afganistɑ̃]
Bangladesh	**Bangladesh** (m)	[bɑ̃gladɛʃ]
Indonesia	**Indonésie** (f)	[ɛ̃dɔnezi]
Jordan	**Jordanie** (f)	[ʒɔrdani]

Iraq	**Iraq** (m)	[irak]
Iran	**Iran** (m)	[irɑ̃]
Cambodia	**Cambodge** (m)	[kɑ̃bɔdʒ]
Kuwait	**Koweït** (m)	[kɔwɛjt]

Laos	**Laos** (m)	[laos]
Myanmar	**Myanmar** (m)	[mjanmar]
Nepal	**Népal** (m)	[nepal]
United Arab Emirates	**Fédération** (f) **des Émirats Arabes Unis**	[federasjɔ̃ dezemira arabzyni]

Syria	**Syrie** (f)	[siri]
Palestine	**Palestine** (f)	[palɛstin]
South Korea	**Corée** (f) **du Sud**	[kɔre dy syd]
North Korea	**Corée** (f) **du Nord**	[kɔre dy nɔr]

151. North America

United States of America	**les États Unis**	[lezeta zyni]
Canada	**Canada** (m)	[kanada]
Mexico	**Mexique** (m)	[mɛksik]

152. Central and South America

Argentina	**Argentine** (f)	[arʒɑ̃tin]
Brazil	**Brésil** (m)	[brezil]
Colombia	**Colombie** (f)	[kɔlɔ̃bi]
Cuba	**Cuba** (f)	[kyba]
Chile	**Chili** (m)	[ʃili]

Bolivia	**Bolivie** (f)	[bɔlivi]
Venezuela	**Venezuela** (f)	[venezɥela]
Paraguay	**Paraguay** (m)	[paragwɛ]
Peru	**Pérou** (m)	[peru]

| Suriname | **Surinam** (m) | [syrinam] |
| Uruguay | **Uruguay** (m) | [yrygwɛ] |

Ecuador	Équateur (m)	[ekwatœr]
The Bahamas	Bahamas (f pl)	[baamas]
Haiti	Haïti (m)	[aiti]

Dominican Republic	République (f) Dominicaine	[repyblik dɔminikɛn]
Panama	Panamá (m)	[panama]
Jamaica	Jamaïque (f)	[ʒamaik]

153. Africa

Egypt	Égypte (f)	[eʒipt]
Morocco	Maroc (m)	[marɔk]
Tunisia	Tunisie (f)	[tynizi]

Ghana	Ghana (m)	[gana]
Zanzibar	Zanzibar (m)	[zɑ̃zibar]
Kenya	Kenya (m)	[kenja]
Libya	Libye (f)	[libi]
Madagascar	Madagascar (f)	[madagaskar]

Namibia	Namibie (f)	[namibi]
Senegal	Sénégal (m)	[senegal]
Tanzania	Tanzanie (f)	[tɑ̃zani]
South Africa	République (f) Sud-africaine	[repyblik sydafrikɛn]

154. Australia. Oceania

| Australia | Australie (f) | [ostrali] |
| New Zealand | Nouvelle Zélande (f) | [nuvɛl zelɑ̃d] |

| Tasmania | Tasmanie (f) | [tasmani] |
| French Polynesia | Polynésie (f) Française | [pɔlinezi frɑ̃sɛz] |

155. Cities

Amsterdam	Amsterdam (f)	[amstɛrdam]
Ankara	Ankara (m)	[ɑ̃kara]
Athens	Athènes (m)	[atɛn]
Baghdad	Bagdad (m)	[bagdad]
Bangkok	Bangkok (m)	[bɑ̃kɔk]
Barcelona	Barcelone (f)	[barsələn]

| Beijing | Pékin (m) | [pekɛ̃] |
| Beirut | Beyrouth (m) | [berut] |

Berlin	**Berlin** (m)	[bɛrlɛ̃]
Bombay, Mumbai	**Bombay** (m)	[bɔ̃bɛ]
Bonn	**Bonn** (f)	[bɔn]
Bordeaux	**Bordeaux** (f)	[bordo]
Bratislava	**Bratislava** (m)	[bratislava]
Brussels	**Bruxelles** (m)	[brysɛl]
Bucharest	**Bucarest** (m)	[bykarɛst]
Budapest	**Budapest** (m)	[bydapɛst]
Cairo	**Caire** (m)	[kɛr]
Calcutta	**Calcutta** (f)	[kalkyta]
Chicago	**Chicago** (f)	[ʃikago]
Copenhagen	**Copenhague** (f)	[kɔpənag]
Dar-es-Salaam	**Dar es-Salaam** (f)	[darɛssalam]
Delhi	**Delhi** (f)	[deli]
Dubai	**Dubaï** (f)	[dybaj]
Dublin	**Dublin** (f)	[dyblɛ̃]
Düsseldorf	**Düsseldorf** (f)	[dysɛldɔrf]
Florence	**Florence** (f)	[flɔrɑ̃s]
Frankfurt	**Francfort** (f)	[frɑ̃kfɔr]
Geneva	**Genève** (f)	[ʒənɛv]
The Hague	**Hague** (f)	[ag]
Hamburg	**Hambourg** (f)	[ɑ̃bur]
Hanoi	**Hanoi** (f)	[anɔj]
Havana	**Havane** (f)	[avan]
Helsinki	**Helsinki** (f)	[ɛlsiŋki]
Hiroshima	**Hiroshima** (f)	[iroʃima]
Hong Kong	**Hong Kong** (m)	[ɔ̃gkɔ̃g]
Istanbul	**Istanbul** (f)	[istɑ̃bul]
Jerusalem	**Jérusalem** (f)	[ʒeryzalɛm]
Kiev	**Kiev** (f)	[kjɛf]
Kuala Lumpur	**Kuala Lumpur** (f)	[kwalalumpur]
Lisbon	**Lisbonne** (f)	[lizbɔn]
London	**Londres** (m)	[lɔ̃dr]
Los Angeles	**Los Angeles** (f)	[lɔsɑ̃dʒəlɛs]
Lyons	**Lyon** (f)	[ljɔ̃]
Madrid	**Madrid** (f)	[madrid]
Marseille	**Marseille** (f)	[marsɛj]
Mexico City	**Mexico** (f)	[mɛksiko]
Miami	**Miami** (f)	[miami]
Montreal	**Montréal** (f)	[mɔ̃real]
Moscow	**Moscou** (f)	[mɔsku]
Munich	**Munich** (f)	[mynik]
Nairobi	**Nairobi** (f)	[nɛrɔbi]
Naples	**Naples** (f)	[napl]

New York	**New York** (f)	[nujɔrk]
Nice	**Nice** (f)	[nis]
Oslo	**Oslo** (m)	[ɔslo]
Ottawa	**Ottawa** (m)	[ɔtawa]
Paris	**Paris** (m)	[pari]
Prague	**Prague** (m)	[prag]
Rio de Janeiro	**Rio de Janeiro** (m)	[rijodədʒanɛro]
Rome	**Rome** (f)	[rɔm]
Saint Petersburg	**Saint-Pétersbourg** (m)	[sɛ̃petɛrsbur]
Seoul	**Séoul** (m)	[seul]
Shanghai	**Shanghai** (m)	[ʃɑ̃gaj]
Singapore	**Singapour** (f)	[sɛ̃gapur]
Stockholm	**Stockholm** (m)	[stɔkɔlm]
Sydney	**Sidney** (m)	[sidnɛ]
Taipei	**Taipei** (m)	[tajbɛj]
Tokyo	**Tokyo** (m)	[tɔkjo]
Toronto	**Toronto** (m)	[tɔrɔ̃to]
Venice	**Venise** (f)	[vəniz]
Vienna	**Vienne** (f)	[vjɛn]
Warsaw	**Varsovie** (f)	[varsɔvi]
Washington	**Washington** (f)	[waʃiŋtɔn]

CPSIA information can be obtained
at www.ICGtesting.com
Printed in the USA
FFOW04n0855011215
19160FF